CLASSICAL MYTHOLOGY
IN THE
POETRY OF EDMUND SPENSER

CLASSICAL MYTHOLOGY

IN THE

POETRY OF EDMUND SPENSER

A DISSERTATION SUBMITTED TO THE ENGLISH
FACULTY OF PRINCETON UNIVERSITY IN PAR-
TIAL FULFILLMENT OF THE REQUIREMENTS
FOR THE DEGREE OF DOCTOR OF PHILOSOPHY

BY

HENRY GIBBONS LOTSPEICH
Instructor in English
Princeton University

PRINCETON STUDIES IN ENGLISH
NUMBER 9

NEW YORK
GORDIAN PRESS, INC.
1965

Originally published 1932
Reprinted 1965

Library of Congress Catalog Card Number 65-28856

Printed in U.S.A. by
Edwards Brothers, Inc.
Ann Arbor, Michigan

·PREFACE

THIS study began as an attempt to supplement the work done by Dr. Alice E. Sawtelle in her *The Sources of Spenser's Classical Mythology*. As a guide and as groundwork, her book has been of very great assistance. It became apparent, however, that the subject demanded fuller treatment than she was able to give it. The range of Spenser's mythology was found to be broader and more varied than that indicated by her dictionary. There was need of a general estimate of the significance of classic myth in Spenser's poetry. There was also the need to reëxamine the whole question of the sources which he used. On this subject Dr. Sawtelle said: "Although in certain minor details he may have been indebted to intermediate authorities, like Natalis Comes . . . or to other poets of the Middle Ages, yet there is every evidence, from the paraphrasing of the Greek and Latin and from the vital, original spirit breathing through the mythological passages, that he drew his inspiration directly from the fountain-heads" (pages 8, 9). That Spenser did go to the fountain-heads, especially Latin ones, is quite plain. I have tried to show in some detail his indebtedness to the classics for mythical material and poetic phrase. But I have also, I hope, established the importance of other sources as well; and among these the books of Boccaccio and Natalis Comes stand first. Spenser is indebted to them for a great deal more than minor details. They supplied him, in large measure, with the material of myth; they shaped his conception of its meaning and its possibilities, and they were, in many instances, the media through which he found his way back to the fountain-heads. Source study of Spenser is a complex matter in which the certainty of final conclusions is hard to attain; but in the matter of classical mythology it seems clear that his sources were much more numerous and various than Dr. Sawtelle indicated, including, in addition to the

Latin and some Greek classics, not only Boccaccio and Comes, but also Petrarch, Ronsard, Du Bellay, Chaucer, Sackville, and others.

In making the apparatus of the dictionary, I have depended very largely on the Concordance and on Whitman's *Subject-Index*. With two such works of reference easily accessible, I have thought it unnecessary, in the case of the longer articles, to give exhaustive references to Spenser's text. References are complete wherever they can be so without cumbersomeness. Elsewhere, my method has been selective.

My debt to Spenser's editors and critics in general is, by the nature of the work, a large one. I have tried to acknowledge it in detail at the appropriate points.

My work was begun at the suggestion of Professor Charles G. Osgood and has been carried on under his guidance. My debt to him, for the benefit of his insight into Spenser and for his unfailing helpfulness and kindness, is one which I cannot adequately acknowledge.

H. G. L.

TABLE OF ABBREVIATIONS

Aen.	Vergil, *Aeneid*
Am.	*Amoretti*
Ant. Rome	Du Bellay, *Les Antiquitez de Rome* (*Œuvres Pōetiques*, ed. Chamard, 2.3–29)
Apollod.	Apollodorus, *Bibliotheca*
Ap. Rh.	Apollonius Rhodius, *Argonautica*
Ast.	*Astrophel*
Bocc.	Boccaccio, *De Genealogia Deorum Gentilium* (1st ed., Venice, 1472; ed. used, Basel, 1532)
Burmann	Petrus Burmannus, ed., *P. Ovidii Nasonis Metamorphoseon Libri XV*, Amsterdam, 1727 (includes the notes of Regius, Micyllus, and others)
CCCHA	*Colin Clouts Come Home Againe*
Claudian, *R.P.*	Claudian, *De Raptu Proserpinae*
Daph.	*Daphnaida*
Ded. Son.	Dedicatory Sonnets prefaced to *The Faerie Queene*
Diodorus	Diodorus Siculus, *Bibliotheca Historica*
Dodge	R. E. N. Dodge, *The Complete Poetical Works of Edmund Spenser*, Student's Cambridge Edition, Boston, 1908
Ecl.	Vergil, *Eclogues*
Emerson	O. F. Emerson, "Spenser's Virgils Gnat," *JEGP*,17.94–118
Epig.	*Epigrams* (appended to the *Amoretti*)
Epith.	*Epithalamion*
F.Q.	*The Faerie Queene*
Fulgentius	Fulgentius, *Mitologiarum Libri Tres* (ed. Teubner, 1898)
Geo.	Vergil, *Georgics*
Gough	*The Faerie Queene*, Book Five, ed. A. B. Gough, Oxford, 1921

H.L.	*An Hymne in Honour of Love*
H.B.	*An Hymne in Honour of Beautie*
H.H.L.	*An Hymne of Heavenly Love*
H.H.B.	*An Hymne of Heavenly Beautie*
Harper	Carrie A. Harper, *The Sources of British Chronicle History in Spenser's 'Faerie Queene,'* Philadelphia, 1910
Hughes	M. Y. Hughes, *Virgil and Spenser*, U. of Cal. Publications in English, vol. 2, no. 3, Berkeley, 1929
Hygin., *Fab.*	Hyginus, *Fabularum Liber* (in *Auctores Mythographi Latini*, ed. A. van Staveren, Amsterdam, 1742)
Hygin., *P.A.*	Hyginus, *Poeticum Astronomicum* (also in *Auctores* . . .)
Il.	Homer, *Iliad*
Lact.	Lactantius Placidus, *Commentary on Statius* (ed. Teubner, 1898)
Lee	R. W. Lee, *Platonism in Spenser*, Princeton Ms. Diss., 1926. (I refer to this without citing page numbers since, when it appears in print, the paging will have changed.)
Lemmi	C. W. Lemmi, "The Symbolism of the Classical Episodes in *The Faerie Queene*," *Phil. Quarterly*, 8.270–87
M.H.T.	*Mother Hubberds Tale*
Met.	Ovid, *Metamorphoses*
Mui.	*Muiopotmos*
Mustard	W. P. Mustard, "E.K.'s Classical Allusions," *MLN*, 34.193–203
Mut.	*Mutabilitie* (*The Faerie Queene*, Bk. VII)
N.C.	Natalis Comes, *Mythologiae; sive, explicationum Fabularum Libri X* (1st ed. Venice, 1551; ed. used, Lyon, 1602)
Od.	Homer, *Odyssey*

Osgood

C. G. Osgood, *Boccaccio on Poetry*, Being the Preface and the Fourteenth and Fifteenth Books of Boccaccio's *Genealogia Deorum Gentilium*, Princeton, 1930

Osgood, *Milton*

C. G. Osgood, *The Classical Mythology of Milton's English Poems, Yale Studies in English VIII*, New York, 1900

Plésent

Le Culex, ed. Charles Plésent, Paris, 1910

Proth.

Prothalamion

R.R.

The Ruines of Rome

R.T.

The Ruines of Time

Renwick, *Compl.*

W. L. Renwick, ed. *Complaints*, London, 1928

Renwick, *Daph.*

W. L. Renwick, ed. *Daphnaida and Other Poems*, London, 1929

Renwick, *S.C.*

W. L. Renwick, ed. *The Shepherd's Calendar*, London, 1930

Riedner

Wilhelm Riedner, *Spensers Belesenheit, Münchener Beiträge zur Romanischen und Englischen Philologie*, vol. 38, Leipzig, 1908

Roscher

Ausführliches Lexikon der Griechischen und Römischen Mythologie, ed. W. H. Roscher, Leipzig, 1884–90

S.

Alice E. Sawtelle, *The Sources of Spenser's Classical Mythology*, Boston, 1896

S.C.

The Shepheardes Calender

Servius

Servii Grammatici qui feruntur in Vergilii Carmina Commentarii, ed. Thilo and Hagen, Leipzig, 1881

Silvae

Statius, *Silvae*

Songe

Du Bellay, *Songe* (*Œuvres Poétiques*, ed Chamard, 2.30–39)

Sp.

Edmund Spenser

T. M.

The Teares of the Muses

Theb.

Statius, *Thebaid*

Theog.

Hesiod, *Theogony*

Todd	*The Works of Edmund Spenser* . . . with the Principal Illustrations of Various Commentators, ed. H. J. Todd, London, 1805 (References to Warton, Jortin, and Upton are to their notes in Todd.)
V.B.	*The Visions of Bellay*
V.G.	*Virgils Gnat*
V.P.	*The Visions of Petrarch*
Van Winkle	C. Van Winkle, ed. *Epithalamion*, New York, 1926
V.W.V.	*Visions of the Worlds Vanity*
Whitman	C. H. Whitman, *A Subject-Index to the Poems of Edmund Spenser*, New Haven, 1918
Winst., *F.Q. I*	Lilian Winstanley, ed. *The Faerie Queene*, Book I, Cambridge, 1924
Winst., *F.Q. II*	Lilian Winstanley, ed. *The Faerie Queene*, Book II, Cambridge, 1922
Winst., *Hymnes*	Lilian Winstanley, ed. *The Fowre Hymnes*, Cambridge, 1916

INTRODUCTION

I

WHILE Sir Calidore, the knight of Courtesy, is pursuing the
Blatant Beast through cities and courts and even into "the
open fields," he chances on a bit of Arcadia, where shepherds are

> singing to their flockes . . .
> Layes of sweete love and youthes delightfull heat.

They know nothing of the Beast with the thousand lying tongues,
but they offer him drink and homely food, and Calidore stops to
rest. On a little hillock nearby, a shepherdess is sitting, clad in
homemade green, her head crowned with a garland. The "lustie
shepheard swaines" sit before her and pipe and sing her praises. Sir
Calidore forgets his quest and falls in love with Pastorella.

The "sage and serious" poet seems to be forgetting his business.
His hero is far from the works which should show his mettle, and
the *bête noire* of Courtesy is rampant. But Spenser has not forgotten
his business. He takes this period of rest between activities to show
us a vision of ideal Courtesy; and into the vision he weaves reminiscences of his own experience, experience which has bound him
with personal ties to the cause of all true courtiers and lovers. For
the substance of his vision he turns to classic myth.

One day, while Calidore is wandering in the fields, "far from all
peoples troad," he comes

> Unto a place, whose pleasaunce did appere
> To passe all others on the earth which were.

It is a hill, covered with trees which bud in winter as in summer, a
place where Nature has heaped all her riches. From it flows a silver
stream, where "the ruder clowne" may not approach, but only
nymphs and fairies. It is called Mount Acidale, the haunt of the
Graces, the place that Venus loves even more than her royal court
at Cytheron. On the hill's top is a broad plain and there Calidore
hears the sound of dancing and singing. He goes near and hides
himself at the edge of an open glade. Before him he sees

> An hundred naked maidens lilly white,
> All raunged in a ring, and dauncing in delight.

Within the ring are three other ladies, the Graces themselves, "the daughters of sky-ruling Jove," who "on men all gracious gifts bestow, which decke the body or adorne the minde," who teach men "all the complements of curtesie." In the center, encircled as with a garland more fair than Ariadne's crown, is "another damzell," a fourth Grace, outshining all the rest as a gem does its setting. Before them sits a shepherd, piping, but his music is only for that other Grace, for the shepherd is "poore Colin Clout" and the lady is that "shepheards lasse" of whom he sang long ago, whom he has called up again before his eyes with the power of his music.

Sir Calidore stands for a while in wonder and then steps out into the glade. As soon as he appears, the vision is gone. Colin must console himself with explaining to the knight who these ladies were.

To one who is not acquainted with Spenser's ways, it is probably surprising to come upon Mount Acidale and three Greek goddesses in an English and Irish Fairyland. The whole episode is typically Spenserian. The poet is talking about Courtesy. The Graces fit his purpose, because, in the hands of commentators, they have come to stand for Courtesy in the Elizabethan sense. The allegorical meaning attached to myth goes far, as we shall see, in explaining Spenser's use of such material throughout his work. The ideal of the learned poet also explains much. He must dignify his verse even with allusions within allusions, so to speak, such as the one here about Ariadne's crown. But the whole thing goes deeper than allegory or learned allusion. Spenser's personal feeling for things is the most compelling reason. In this episode Spenser is writing about his own lady, "there advaunst to be another Grace." Classic myth, plastic and adaptable, has been woven around his own love affair. Somehow, this mythology, learned from books and from fellow-poets, has come to mean so much to him that he can speak in its idiom when he comes to touch on the most intimate of his own experiences. Perhaps we can get no farther in explaining why Colin Clout is singing on Mount Acidale.

The meaning which Spenser found in classic myth, like the meaning he found in most things, is rich and many-sided. One can never be sure that one has seen it all. Some of it, in more detail, will emerge as we examine the various ways in which Spenser uses myth; but there is one general idea which is basic to the whole matter. We, now, have a habit of considering mythology as something separate and circumscribed, a body of anonymous lore, with its roots in popular belief. Not so Spenser. Myth and poetry were, in his mind, one and the same; the ancient poets were the myth-makers, and the myth-makers were poets. Thus E. K. habitually speaks of myths as the "inventions" of the poets[1] and Spenser himself says that "the antique wisards" or antiquity "invented" the myths of Venus' birth, of Agdistes, of Love, and of Osiris.[2] The Muses made Hercules and Bacchus immortal,[3] which is a way of saying that the poets, by perpetuating their fame, made them into figures of myth.

Several factors were at work, in Spenser's case, to make for this equation of poetry and myth. There was, first and foremost, his instinct as a poet, which showed him the poetic qualities inherent in any mythology. There was also the tradition which he inherited. He took his myth from two main sources: from classical authors, in whose hands it had already become poetry, and from compendiums which treated poetry and myth as interchangeable terms.[4] Thus Spenser was in a tradition which regarded myth as an essential substance of poetry, as one with it.

This identification of poetry and myth goes far in explaining the very integral and inseparable part which classical mythology plays in the world of Spenser's poetry. It would be hard to state how completely and organically this classical material has been woven into the fabric of romance. Muses and nymphs and fairies dance to-

[1] See glosses on April 41, July 59, 64, 77, 154; Nov. 141, 179. One contributing factor in this identification of poetry and myth was the theory that ancient poetry had originated in religion, and that the first poets were theologians, whence later poets were called *vates*. This is in Bocc. 14.8, where Sp. may have seen it; cf. Osgood, pp. 42–46 and 162–63, where he shows the same idea in Aristotle and Augustine and others, and cf. also Osgood, pp. 121–23, 194–95.
[2] *F.Q.* 2.12.48; 3.3.2; 4.12.2; 5.7.2.
[3] *T.M.* 461–2; cf. *R.T.* 372, f.
[4] See Osgood, pp. xvi, 47–54, 85. The same identification is found throughout N.C., who refers to poets and myth-makers, without distinction, as the "antiqui"; cf. *Cupid, Scylla*.

gether.[5] Satyrs are near at hand to rescue Una from Sansloy.[6] Cupid holds a masque in a medieval castle.[7] Tristram of Lionesse lives among the nymphs, who come to him "as they were wont unto Latonaes sonne."[8] No English poet has made classic myth so completely at home. A study of Spenser's use of classic myth will show how an important foreign tradition has become organic in poetry which is essentially English; and it will show also that Spenser's ideal of poetry knows no distinctions of time or place, and that his achievement is large enough to include within itself materials drawn from widely separate quarters, the "sweet variety" of many different lands and places, the "rare thoughts" of many different poets and peoples.

Consideration of the ways in which Spenser uses classic myth falls into two main parts: first, myth used as ornament, in a large sense of that word, as part of the surface beauty of poetry and as part of the narrative or "fable"; and, second, myth used to express what lies beneath the fable, what constitutes, again in a large sense, the allegory.

II

The Faerie Queene employs all the stylistic and rhetorical devices of the full-dress epic. Anyone, in Spenser's day, who set out to do for England what Vergil had done for Rome would naturally seek to dignify his poem with all the ornamentation traditionally associated with the high style. The critical doctrines which Spenser followed demanded ornateness.[9] In his work, the major part of such ornamentation is drawn from classical mythology. It may appear in various ways: in brief and somewhat learned allusions, in references to Aurora and Phoebus to punctuate the passing of time, in similes. These are some of the ways in which classic myth contributes to the surface beauty of his poetry.

---

[5] See *S.C.* May 32–3, June 25–8; *T.M.* 31; 6.10.7, 17; cf. E.K. on April 120. See *Nymphs*.
[6] *F.Q.* 1.6.7, f.   [7] *F.Q.* 3.12.3, f.   [8] *F.Q.* 6.2.25.
[9] Cf. Du Bellay, *Déffense et Illustration de la Langue Francayse*, ed. Séché, pp. 126-7: "Sur toutes choses, prends garde que ce genre de poëme soit elongné du vulgaire, enrichy et illustré de mots propres et epithètes non oisifs, orné de graves sentences et varié de toutes manières de couleurs et ornements poëtiques."

Spenser showed his tastes early, when he translated the Vergilian *Culex*. In it he found an example of that kind of late classical poetry in which mythological ornateness abounds and which is especially characterized by the remote and learned allusion made fashionable by the Alexandrians. *Virgils Gnat* is, as Renwick says, "one large literary allusion."[10] The very simple trifle which forms its plot is padded out with some three hundred and fifty lines of incidental and episodic material, nearly all drawn from classic myth.

The influence of this early translation on Spenser's later work, demonstrable in several matters of detail,[11] is certainly in part responsible for his habit of using the indirect, learned allusion. Thus he is following the Alexandrian manner when he refers to Proserpina as "the Thracian maid" (leaving the reader to explain it if he can), or to Hercules as the "Tirynthian groom." The whole story of Narcissus is suggested in the line,

> Foolish Narcisse that likes the watry shore. (3.6.45)

A longer passage in which suggestiveness and the invitation to learned comment are combined is that on the Sea-Gods.[12] The poet assumes that his reader will know all about

> Phorcys, the father of that fatall brood,
> By whom those old heroes wonne such fame.

This use of allusions which presuppose a learned reader may serve to remind us that Spenser's poetry is aristocratic, that it is addressed to the few who were at once courtier, scholar, soldier.

In the high style it has long been conventional to mark the passing of time by mythological references. Aurora, Phoebus, and Cynthia are the accepted periphrases for the dawn, the sun, and the moon. This rather threadbare device was already well-worn in Spenser's time. Sometimes Spenser merely echoes an earlier poet,

[10] W. L. Renwick, *Edmund Spenser, An Essay on Renaissance Poetry*, p. 57.
[11] At two points in *F.Q.* the influence of *V.G.* seems quite clear: 1.5.34, describing Cerberus (cf. *V.G.* 345–52), and 2.12.6, on Charybdis and Tartarus (cf. *V.G.* 541–3); see *Cerberus, Tartarus*. There are numerous other cases where *V.G.* at least offers the same material as is found in later allusions, although direct influence cannot be proved. See *Agave* 2, *Castalia, Cimmerian Shades, Erebus, Furies, Hesperus, Lethe, Naiads, Narcissus, Oedipus, Orpheus, Parnassus, Phaethon.*
[12] *F.Q.* 4.11.13–14; See *Sea-Gods*.

Vergil, or Homer, or both together.[13] But, habitually, these allusions have a fresh meaning for him and take on new forms. He can skillfully blend literary associations with a fresh record of the thing itself.

> The joyous day gan early to appear,
> And faire Aurora from the deawy bed
> Of aged Tithone gan her selfe to reare,
> With rosy cheekes, for shame as blushing red;
> Her golden locks for hast were loosely shed
> About her eares, when Una her did marke
> Clymbe to her charet, all with flowers spred,
> From heaven high to chace the chearelesse darke;
> With mery note her lowd salutes the mounting larke.

Conventions usually have a reason in the nature of things. Both poetry and myth personify and humanize the phenomena of nature. If the poet really lives through such processes, his use of myth becomes more than conventional. Phoebus, Aurora, and Cynthia may be mere names; and they may stand for something real. The poet who, having stored his mind with literary associations, sees and feels for himself the things which these names symbolize may use the names with more than conventional significance. He may live again the experience of the first myth-makers, who personified the sun and the moon because that was their truly poetic way of conceiving them. It becomes at once conventional and natural for Spenser to say of the moon,

> Who is the same which at my window peepes?
> Or whose is that faire face that shines so bright?
> Is it not Cinthia, she that never sleepes,
> But walkes about high heaven al the night?

And his references to Aurora and Phoebus are fresh and real because he thinks and feels mythologically.

> At last, the golden orientall gate
> Of greatest heaven gan to open fayre,
> And Phoebus, fresh as bridegrome to his mate,
> Came dauncing forth, shaking his deawie hayre,
> And hurld his glistring beams through gloomy ayre. (1.5.2)

---

[13] Cf. *F.Q.* 1.2.7; see *Aurora*.

For our purposes, the most important convention of the high style is the simile. Classic myth has supplied a large share of the material for Spenser's similes. Yet here again, his use of myth is more than conventional. His mythological similes usually have a deeper reason for being. By means of them he is able to point out the kinship between his own heroes and those of classical antiquity. His heroes must appear as the equals of the ancients. Thus the Redcrosse Knight, in his struggles with the dragon, is likened to Hercules;[14] Orgoglio's beast, which Arthur quells, is such a one

> as that renowned snake
> Which great Alcides in Stremona slew, (1.7.17)

and the same struggle is recalled when Sir Calidore finally comes to grips with the Blatant Beast.[15] Again, Calidore, in a particular situation, reminds Spenser of Paris and he is careful to call the reader's attention to the likeness.

> Who had seene him then would have bethought
> On Phrygian Paris by Plexippus brooke,
> When he the love of fayre Oenone sought,
> What time the golden apple was unto him brought. (6.9.36)

Thus similes serve as links connecting Spenser's Fairyland with the world of ancient myth; and the poet's creation gains dignity and authority by the association.

Spenser often goes one step farther in the same direction. He will bring into a simile myth which is, in reality, the source or pattern of the thing he is comparing. The two parts of the simile are in origin the same. For example, he describes Cambina's "rod of peace" and then says that it was "like to the rod which Maias sonne doth wield." The two rods are really one and the same, for the description of Cambina's rod follows closely the description of Mercury's Caduceus in Natalis Comes.[16] Again, describing how Artegal was reduced to effeminacy by Radigund, Spenser compares him to Hercules,

---

[14] *F.Q.* 1.11.27.   [15] *F.Q.* 6.12.32.   [16] See *Caduceus.*

> How for Iolas sake he did apply
> His mightie hands the distaff vile to hold. (5.5.24)

The myth has served as a model for this episode in Artegal's career.[17] Perhaps the most interesting case of this sort is in the description of Geryoneo's monster. Spenser devotes two stanzas to describing the beast and then says,

> Much like in foulnesse and deformity
> Unto that monster whom the Theban knight,
> The father of that fatall progeny,
> Made kill her selfe for very hearts despight,
> That he had red her riddle, which no wight
> Could ever loose, but suffred deadly dole. (5.11.25)

For his picture of his own monster, Spenser has used the description of the Sphinx in Comes.[18] But here the kinship goes further and is one of inner meaning as well as outward form. Geryoneo's monster is, allegorically, the Inquisition; like the Inquisition, the Sphinx poses its riddle, a wrong answer to which means death.

The particular sort of imagination revealed in these examples is found elsewhere as well. We can see it in Spenser's treatment of his semi-mythological characters, Belphoebe and Britomart. Belphoebe is patterned rather closely on Diana and Britomart inherits qualities from Diana and Minerva. Thus the similes are peculiarly appropriate which compare Belphoebe to Diana,[19] and Britomart to Minerva and to Cynthia.[20] Again, Spenser's Lucifera is related to the classical Juno: they both stand for pride. With this in mind, the poet compares the gay coach of Lucifera to

> Great Junoes golden chayre, the which, they say,
> The gods stand gazing on, when she does ride,
> To Joves high hous through heavens bras-paved way,
> Drawne of fayre pecocks, that excell in pride,
> And full of Argus eyes their tayles dispredden wide. (1.4.17).

In such ways, Spenser's mythological similes have a peculiar fitness which results from an inner kinship of character or meaning in the things compared.

[17] See *Iole.*
[18] See *Sphinx, Geryon.*
[19] *F.Q.* 2.3.31; 4.7.30.
[20] *F.Q.* 3.9.22; 3.1.43.

We have already had occasion to touch on the use of myth as source material, but this is a large subject and demands further consideration. Spenser adapts myth and incorporates it into a setting of his own creation. He transforms it and elaborates it and makes it a part of his own narrative. Considering ancient poetry and ancient myth as equivalent and practically the same, he sees in myth poetic raw material to be used quite in the same ways as any purely literaty model might be.

Among Spenser's adaptations from classic myth, some may be grouped together as, in a general way, Ovidian. Whether directly inspired by passages in Ovid or not, they exhibit something of the spirit of the "tenerorum lusor amorum," to whom classic myth was a plaything for his wit and a mine of pretty stories and pictures. In several important instances, where Spenser is using myth almost exclusively for its pictorial value, Ovid is his chief source; and in nearly every case the picture which Spenser creates is more elaborate and vivid than its Ovidian prototype. This is so in the passage on the "clothes of Arras and of Toure" which depict the love of Venus and Adonis,[21] in the more elaborate and splendid tapestries in the hall of Busirane, of Cupid's wars and "all of love and al of lusty-head,"[22] and perhaps most strikingly in the adaptation from Ovid of Minerva's contest with Arachne, in *Muiopotmos*. In this last instance, where Ovid gives five lines to Europa and the bull and then goes on to enumerate twenty other scandalous amours of the gods, Spenser keeps only the episode of Europa and elaborates it into three stanzas of detailed picture. And by the change which Spenser makes in the dénouement of the story, the note of flippant irreverence in Ovid's version is supplanted by a spirit of emulation and pride in the creation of beautiful art.[23]

Spenser also shows himself completely at home in the Ovidian technique of metamorphosis. Following a suggestion from Ovid, he can make up his own, as in the case of Coronis. His manipulation of changes is most skillful in *Muiopotmos*, where one metamorphosis,

[21] *F.Q.* 3.1.34–38.
[22] *F.Q.* 3.11.28–46.
[23] See *Arachne.*

that of Arachne, is from Ovid and the other, that of Astery, is his own creation, developed from certain suggestions in the Psyche myth.[24] In *Muiopotmos* at least, Spenser is taking a holiday from the serious business of the philosophic poet and is using myth as a plaything. Like Ovid, he is seeing the world of mythology as "a free country, wherein the imagination can roam, forming and transforming to suit its pleasure."[25]

In this same lighter vein, and with a surer independence, is the story of Faunus and Molanna, which comes as a pleasant interlude in the midst of the more serious matter of the 'Mutability Cantos. The story is an adaptation of the Actaeon myth, as Spenser found it in Ovid,[26] but it becomes something essentially new. Spenser makes a serio-comic figure of his hero, Faunus, and does away with Ovid's tragic ending. The whole episode is in that vein of playful pleasantry, with just a touch of seriousness, which the Elizabethans controlled supremely well. Spenser's method here is somewhat like that of *Muiopotmos*, but his handling of myth is now more mature, easy, and confident.

Spenser's use of myth as source material for his own creations goes beyond the influence of Ovid or of any one poet. His ways of recreating the material of myth are of various kinds. A complete episode in his narrative may show significant points of similarity with a myth which is not embodied, in its entirety, in any one literary source. Thus the story of Marinell, of his birth and of the care with which he was sheltered by his mother, Cymodoce, has interesting parallels in the myth of Peleus and Thetis and Achilles.[27] Describing the intrigues of Hellenore and Paridell, Spenser clearly has Helen and Paris in mind.[28]

Myth has often helped him in his conception or elaboration of his own characters. Belphoebe and Britomart have already been mentioned. The most patent example is Geryoneo, who is simply a second edition of his father, Geryon. The process is usually more

---

[24] See *Astery 1*.
[25] E. K. Rand, "Ovid and the Spirit of Metamorphosis," *Harvard Essays on Classical Subjects*, p. 234.
[26] See *Actaeon*.   [27] See *Cymodoce*.   [28] See *Helen, Paris*.

subtle and many-sided. Radigund seems to embody memories of Penthesilea, Diodorus' Myrina, and Ariosto's Marfisa, all shaped by Spenser's own ideas of the manly woman. In developing the character and rôle of Mutability, Spenser probably used what Natalis Comes had said about the goddess Fortuna.[29] Sometimes the relationship consists only in a few stray hints. In the episode describing Scudamour in the House of Care,[30] we are now and then reminded of Vulcan and his smiths. We feel that Spenser wants us to think of the Cyclops when he says that the savage man, Lust, had the practice of rolling a stone over the mouth of his cave.[31]

In these various ways Spenser adapts and transforms classic myth in the creation of his narrative. He is using material which is an inseparable part of the large and ancient legacy of literary tradition. The poet who inherited this tradition and worked in its spirit might use it as he would, giving it new life in new settings and moulding it to his own purposes.

III

To the casual reader of Spenser, the uses which he makes of classic myth seem only to corroborate the traditional conception of him as "the poets' poet," who, like his own creation, Clarion, lived among the flowers of the garden, enjoying "delight with liberty." Like any educated Renaissance poet, Spenser decorates his poetry with classical similes, invocations, and graceful allusions to the antique mythology. More than this, we find him turning myth into pictures, portraying the love of Venus and Adonis in "costly clothes of Arras and of Toure," or weaving all the amours of the Olympians into the tapestries on the walls of Busirane's enchanted hall. In all this Spenser appears as the artist of sensuous things, the painter of pictures.

But Spenser did not intend that, in reading his poetry, we should stop with the shows of things. For better or worse, he sought

[29] See *Mutability*.   [30] *F.Q.* 4.5.33, f.   [31] *F.Q.* 4.7.20

to restraine
The lust of lawlesse youth with good advice,

and he wrote a very long poem, which presents, as well as picture and fable, "a continued allegory or darke conceit." I do not propose here to take sides on the question as to whether Spenser was a poet, or a teacher, or both, or neither. A study of his classic myth can, however, be of some help toward an answer to that question. For, in addition to using myth for ornament and picture, Spenser also used it for allegory, especially for shadowing forth the moral doctrines which he considered of the first importance. Of the "fierce warres and faithful loves" which moralize his song, not a little owes its being to the tradition of classic myth as it had been interpreted morally and allegorically by the poets and commentators before him. As an introduction to this part of our subject, we must consider Spenser's indebtedness to the two books which, for him, embodied the tradition of myth interpretation: the *Genealogia Deorum* of Boccaccio and the *Mythologiae* of Natalis Comes.

It has for some time been recognized that Spenser knew and used these two books;[32] but the extent and nature of his indebtedness to them has not before been fully examined. The results of this study show, first of all, that Comes and Boccaccio gave Spenser enough, simply in the way of material, of narrative detail, to allow us to rank them among the poet's major sources.[33] In nu-

---

[32] Warton cited N.C. for the passage on Genius at 2.12.47, f. (Todd 4.207). Upton cited N.C. for the passage on the Sea-Gods, 4.11.13–14 (Todd 5.438), and Bocc. for the references to Jarre and Aeternitie at 2.4.41 (Todd 3.349). In 1884, M. H. Towry ("Spenser and Boccaccio," *The Bibliographer*, London, 5.120) suggested "that the probable source of his mythology was not . . . the classics themselves but Boccaccio's *Genealogy of the Gods* and Natali's *Comes* (sic)." He cited Daemogorgon as evidence of use of Bocc. The matter of Daemogorgon was again noticed by Cornelia C. Coulter ("The Genealogy of the Gods," *Vassar Medieval Studies*, 1923, pp. 315–41), who cited Bocc. also for Sp.'s use of Perseus. Cf. also, on Daemogorgon, Osgood, p. xliv. Miss Sawtelle recognized N.C. as a source for Sp.'s Geryon, Sea-Gods, Titan, and Venus, but did not give references. Frank L. Schoell, "Les Mythologistes Italiens de la Renaissance et la Poésie Elisabéthaine," *Revue de Litt. Comparée*, 1924, pp. 5–25, gave bibliographical material on Bocc. and N.C. and showed the use of N.C. by Chapman. The most important contribution was made by C. W. Lemmi, "The Symbolism of the Classical Episodes in *The Faerie Queene*," *Phil. Quarterly*, 8.270–287. He shows Sp.'s use of N.C. for factual material in two instances (see *Muses, Isis*) and presents a good deal of evidence for his indebtedness to N.C.'s allegorical interpretations. I have incorporated some of his findings: see *Fauns, Golden Chain, Mermaids, Night, Proserpina.*

[33] On Sp.'s indebtedness to N.C. for narrative detail, see *Admetus, Adonis, Aegide, Alcmena, Atalanta, Caduceus, Castor, Cocytus, Danae, Diana, Fates, Founders of Nations, Ganymede, Genius, Geryon, Giants, Graces, Hecate, Hesperides, Hyades, Isis, Lapiths, Litae, Morpheus, Muses, Mutability, Nereids, Nereus, Night, Olympus, Orion, Plenty, Prometheus, Prosperina, Scylla, Sea-Gods, Semele, Sphinx, Tantalus, Tethys, Titan, Venus.* For similar indebtedness to Bocc., see *Achilles, Aeternitie, Alcmena, Avernus, Bellona, Britomart, Chaos, Chloris, Cyparissus, Cytheron, Daemogorgon, Diana, Diomedes, Endymion, Fates, Geryon, Helle, Hercules, Hippolytus, Iole, Jarre, Mars, Muses, Pegasus, Perseus, Theseus, Tryphon, Venus.*

merous instances, when Spenser's version of a myth shows peculiarities which differentiate it from classical versions, authority for, or explanation of, such peculiarities has been found in Comes or Boccaccio. It appears also that some of the material, in its classical form, comes to Spenser, not from the classical texts themselves, but from quotations in these authorities, especially in Comes. We find Spenser, in a number of instances, writing with Comes open before him and following his comments and quotations from classical authors, often keeping the same sequence.[34]

All this does not rule out the influence of the classics used at first hand. That he read much Greek is doubtful; but he does use the Latin poets extensively, especially Vergil and Ovid. What I wish to emphasize here is that the books of Comes and Boccaccio were of the first importance in the transmission of classic myth to Spenser, and that there is enough evidence of his use of them for external material alone to justify us in proceeding to enquire into their influence on his conception of what the ancient myths meant and how they could be used for the purposes of allegory.

Boccaccio and Comes regarded classic myth as a fundamental part of the great and venerable tradition of classical poetry. As such, they often treat it somewhat mystically, as containing hidden meanings of great import. Pagan and frivolous the ancient literature might appear on the surface, but studious insight would show that its creators, even Ovid and Apuleius, were profound speculative and moral philosophers, often inspired by the one God. Boccaccio and Comes did their work in the belief that they were providing keys to the understanding of these hidden meanings. They explain what lies beneath the veil of the fables: the accumulated wisdom of the ancients, their speculations on natural philosophy, their ethical teaching. "This work of mine," says Boccaccio, "removes the veil from these inventions, shows that poets were really men of wisdom, and renders their compositions full of profit and pleasure to the reader."[35] Every myth had a meaning, perhaps

---

[34] See *Adonis, Danae, Ganymede, Genius, Ino, Ixion, Nereids, Nereus, Night, Prometheus, Venus.*
[35] *Genealogia* 15.1; Osgood, p. 105.

several; it was "polyseme," as Boccaccio put it,[36] of many meanings. According to Comes, "the ancient makers of the myths" have
given us, not only their speculations on natural philosophy, but
also, and more important, "the most useful precepts concerning the
life of man." They expressed these truths in the form of myth because they were more pleasant so, easier to remember, and because
they were thus hidden from the vulgar and uneducated. "For, as
wine in badly made jars is corrupted and does not transmit its
pristine sweetness to the drinkers, even so matters divine or philosophical are corrupted by communication with the vulgar, when,
in the course of time, they are passed into ruder hands. Thus it
happens that knowledge of the most important matters, hidden
under the coverings of myth, has been preserved so much the more
intact and has been handed down to posterity."[37]

That all this is quite in agreement with Spenser's own theory of
poetry is fairly obvious. Mythology, as he found it interpreted, was
allegorical. The emphasis was on its inner meaning, especially as
that meaning had to do with morality. Mythology was "polyseme"
and so is Spenser's poetry, especially in such mythological passages
as the Mammon episode, the vision of the Graces on Mount Acidale, and the Mutability Cantos. Specifically, he seems to have in
mind Comes' idea that the sacred truths must be skillfully hidden
and enshrined "beneath the coverings of myth" when he addresses

> Ye sacred imps, that on Parnasso dwell,
> And there the keeping have of learnings threasures,
> Which doe all worldly riches far excell. . . .
> Ne none can find, but who was taught them by the Muse.
>
> Revele to me the sacred noursery
> Of Vertue, which with you doth there remaine. (6.Pr.2,3)

These similarities between the general beliefs of the mythographers and of Spenser indicate that there is a real parallelism between the conception of myth in Boccaccio and Comes and the
conception of epic poetry which appears in the Letter to Raleigh

---

[36] *Genealogia* 1.3; cf. Osgood, p. xvii.
[37] *Mythologiae* 6.6, p. 564.

and underlies the whole *Faerie Queene*. Such agreement in fundamentals leads us to ask this question: can we say that this parallelism goes further and that Spenser believed this classical mythology to be the same kind of allegorical poetry as his own *Faerie Queene*? Did the myths seem to him to express truths allegorically, by fable, and character, and picture, in ways which were already his own? Was mythology really moral truth, "coloured with an historicall fiction," "good discipline, . . . clowdily enwrapped in allegorical devices," and therefore a convenient and worthy vehicle for the fashioning of "a gentleman or noble person in vertuous and gentle discipline?" The answer will rest on a consideration of the nature and extent of Spenser's allegorical use of myth, in so far as it derives from these two books.

Of the traditional modes of interpreting myths, three are used most frequently by both Boccaccio and Comes: the physical, the euhemeristic, and the moral.[38] These three modes are the ones distinguishable in Spenser. Discussion of Spenser's allegorical use of myth can, then, fall into three corresponding divisions, growing, in each instance, from a consideration of his indebtedness to Boccaccio and Comes.

Spenser's use of physical or naturalistic interpretations seems to be the least extensive. One idea, however, should be noticed, a poetic one which enlivens the poet's whole conception of the world of nature. It is the idea, or better, the feeling that there is one great cosmic principle of generation and growth and fertility in the world. This is a favorite with the mythographers and, while Spenser needed no single authority to convince him of its general truth, he does seem to be indebted to Boccaccio and Comes, in several instances, for his use of it.[39] It is in his mind when he speaks of the Nymphs as

> The which in floods and fountaines doe appere,
> And all mankinde do nourish with their waters clere; (4.11.52)

[38] The history of the tradition is told by O. Gruppe, *Geschichte der Klassischen Mythologie*, published as a supplement to Roscher. For a description of these modes of interpretation, see Osgood, pp. xvii–xxv. On Bocc.'s use of them cf. Osgood, pp. xxii–xxv; on N.C. cf. Schoell, *op. cit.* p. 14.

[39] See *Apollo, Hours, Neptune, Nymphs, Ocean*, where he uses N.C.; see *Hebe, Ops, Zephirus, Zodiac*, where he uses Bocc. For the physical interpretation see also *Cupid, Mutability*.

and when he speaks of the Ocean's "fruitful froth," and when he says of Apollo,

> Great father he of generation
> Is rightly cald, th'authour of life and light. (3.6.9)

The same idea controls most of his treatment of Venus, about whom we shall have something to say later.

Euhemerism, which originated as a way of explaining how human beings came, in various unenlightened ways, to be worshipped as gods,[40] is used by Boccaccio and Comes with different effect. With them it is a way of making the gods seem more like real people. They show that the fables are real because in them lies historical truth. This conception of the historical nature of myth manifests itself in Spenser in several ways; and, in several cases, the influence of Boccaccio and Comes is demonstrable.[41] For example, Comes gives a full and circumstantial account of Bacchus' human activities as a conqueror and a peace-maker. Bacchus appears in these capacities, along with Hercules and Artegal, at the beginning of Book Five. E. K. says that Atlas was a king who gained his reputation by his skill in finding out "the hidden courses of the starres by an excellent imagination." This interpretation is in Boccaccio and Comes and others. Boccaccio looks upon the whole Aeneas myth as the true history of the founding of Rome. The manner in which Spenser introduces the same story into one of his passages on the ancestry of Britomart and the origins of England shows that he also is considering it as history. Perhaps the clearest case of euhemerism in Spenser is in what he says of Osiris:

> Well therefore did the antique world invent,
> That Justice was a god of soveraine grace,
> And altars unto him, and temples lent,
> And heavenly honors in the highest place;
> Calling him great Osyris, of the race
> Of th'old Ægyptian kings, that whylome were;
> With fayned colours shading a true case:

[40] Cf. D. H. Cooke, "Euhemerism," *Speculum*, 2.396–410.
[41] See *Aeneas, Atlas, Bacchus.*

For that Osyris, whilest he lived here,
The justest man alive and truest did appeare. (5.7.2)

Thus the gods, viewed from one angle, were real human beings, who attained divinity because of their virtue or because they were immortalized by the poets.

The euhemeristic tendency has further ramifications in Spenser. The conception of the gods as real people, thus supported by tradition, helps to explain how they become natural members of Spenser's world and are on terms of every-day familiarity with his own heroes and heroines. It lies behind the episode of Cymodoce and Marinell, which we have already noticed, and it is implicit in his treatment of such characters of mythological origin as Belphoebe, Britomart, Proteus, and Talus. It may also help to explain Spenser's practice of connecting his own characters genealogically with those of myth, as in the case of Satyrane, and of having them educated by the gods, as were Amoret and Belphoebe, Florimel, and Artegal.

The Renaissance commentators lay most emphasis on the moralistic interpretation of myth. In contrast with the medieval habit of astrologizing the gods and of referring their significance to supernatural causes, Boccaccio, and more especially Comes, are most interested in the human, moral implications of the myths. Comes' interpretations are always fullest when he is explaining "the most useful precepts concerning the life of man," or, in the phrase which he uses repeatedly, "quod attinet ad mores." This shift of emphasis involves, with them, a more humanistic conception of life, a recognition that man's destiny is largely in his own hands, an interest, less in supernatural forces, planetary or other, than in men and morality. Spenser's dominant concern throughout *The Faerie Queene*, even in the Legend of Holiness, is ethical: the problem of the good life here and now. The moralistic treatment of myth in Comes and Boccaccio is, therefore, of the first importance. Among the teachers of morality to whom Spenser turned, these two should have place with Plato, Aristotle, Castiglione, and the rest.[42]

---

[42] For Sp.'s use of N.C.'s moral interpretations, see *Argonautica, Astraea, Deucalion, Fauns, Genius, Golden Chain, Helen, Ignorance, Juno, Mermaids, Paris, Phaethon, Pluto, Proserpina, Satyrs, Scylla,*

Perhaps because of the nature of the theme, formal moral allegory is most prominent in the Book of Temperance, or Continence. The two most important allegorical passages in the book draw heavily on classic myth: the Mammon episode and the episode of the Bowre of Blis. In the Mammon episode,[43] materials from many different sources are brought together and are held together by the bond of the allegorical meaning which they are intended to shadow forth. From moral considerations in which Comes and Boccaccio have had a share, the mood of "the divine Vergilian pity" has gone out of the conception of Hades and it has become Hell, a place of terror, an allegory of the temptations and punishments of sinners.[44] The interpretation of Pluto as the avaricious god of wealth, found in both Comes and Boccaccio, has influenced Spenser's conception of Mammon.[45] The famous Golden Chain of Homer had been made by Comes into a symbol of ambition and avarice; Spenser brings it into Philotime's court and labels it "Ambition."[46] The golden apples in Proserpina's garden, with the meaning attached to them by Comes, become symbols of the temptations to which Guyon is being subjected.[47] Branded by the same commentators as a type of avarice, Tantalus finds his place there,[48] so that Guyon can wag his finger at him and say,

---

Tantalus, Titans. For his use of Bocc's moral interpretations, see *Achilles, Ammon, Antaeus, Biblis, Celaeno, Fame, Flora, Graces, Hades, Juno, Mermaids, Paris, Pasiphae, Phlegethon, Proteus, Psyche, Tantalus.*

[43] *F.Q.* 2.7.3, f.

[44] Hughes, pp. 371–81, makes the point that the "mood of reverent pity for the dead and of curious, speculative faith hardly distinguishable from doubt about the immortality of the soul," which pervades Vergil's Hades is not recaptured by Sp. where he is working from passages in *Aeneid* 6. In its place is "stark allegory," the prevailing note of which is one of horror. There is a germ of this in the Vergilian passages which lie behind 2.7.21–23 (*Aen.* 6.280–1, 285–9).) But the difference between Vergil's Hades and Sp.'s is mainly the result of the intrusion of moral allegory for which Sp. found his authority in Bocc. and N.C. N.C., discussing the intent of the ancients in their mythology of the infernal regions, says, "Many terrible things in the lower regions and things *horrenda dictu* have been imagined, by which to lead ruder men into virtue" (3, Proem). Bocc. has the same idea in a passage which has probably influenced 2.7.21–23 (see *Hades*). Cf. also *Acheron, Cocytus, Phlegethon.* Thus the classical Hades had become, for Sp., an allegory which was to teach virtue by inspiring fear. The conception of Hades as filled with personifications and representations of evil is probably again in his mind when he has such monsters as the Blatant Beast, "bred of hellish strene And long in darkesome Stygian den upbrought" (6.6.9).

[45] See *Pluto.*

[46] See *Golden Chain.*

[47] See *Proserpina.*

[48] See *Tantalus.*

'Nay, nay, thou greedy Tantalus, . . .
Abide the fortune of thy present fate,
And unto all that live in high degree
Ensample be of mind intemperate,
To teach them how to use their present state.' (2.7.60)

In the canto on the Bowre of Blis, Spenser makes use of all the
moral symbolism and allegory that had grown up in commentary
on the voyages of Ulysses, Jason, and Aeneas. It will not do to con-
fine Spenser to one source, especially in an episode like this one;
but it seems clear that here as elsewhere, the mythographers, especially Comes, supplied him with much of his symbolism, and
with its meaning made ready to his hand. Comes had said that the
myth of Jason and Medea exemplified "voluptatum desiderium";[49]
Spenser has the story, "framed of precious ivory," over the entrance of Acrasia's garden. As Warton noticed long ago, the description of Genius, or Agdistes, comes bodily from Comes. Quite
as important as Comes' description of this figure is his statement
that Genius leads men into error and lust with dreams and false
spectacles.[50] In his description of the Mermaids, or Sirens, the poet
draws again on Comes,[51] and not very far in the background is
Comes' allegory: "I believe the Sirens' song and the Sirens themselves to be nothing other than voluptuous desire." For the poet's
allegorical use of the voyage between rocks and whirlpools, Comes'
chapter on Scylla and Charybdis was an important precedent.[52]
From it Spenser has taken several descriptive details and in it he
found a full statement of his own moral allegory, expressed in his
own figurative idiom. By the navigator who sails between Scylla
and Charybdis and finally emerges in safety, "what else is meant
but that which is written by Aristotle in his *Ethics*, that virtue is
the mean between two extremes, both of which must be avoided?
. . . What is life but a diligent and continuous voyage among various temptations and illegitimate desires? If a man approaches near
to any of these rocks, he must keep away from them with all his
strength; for there is no man who is not naturally excited by sensual

[49] See *Argonautica*.
[50] See *Genius*.
[51] See *Mermaids*.
[52] See *Scylla*.

pleasures. . . . Thus the ancients wished to show that life is most full of hardships and perils, like a voyage between two terrible rocks; and unless this is most wisely guided, men are caught by voluptuous desire and fall into the most wretched miseries. This of Scylla and Charybdis, which the ancients clothed in the most pleasing tales and fables."

I think it is clear from such evidence that the parallelism in question is fairly close. The mythographers did more than collect the data of ancient myth and present for the poet's use treasuries of the symbol of ancient literature. By interpreting this mythology in the light of ideas which fitted Spenser's deeper purposes, they afforded him a body of poetic allegory already adapted to his own ends. The ways of Boccaccio and Comes in handling the myths were Spenser's ways in shadowing forth his own "darke conceits." Whether, in given cases where he is using classic myth, he took over their interpretations, or made up his own, he is following them in spirit.

The organic and important part which classic myth plays as an expression of Spenser's allegory thus owes a great deal to the work of Boccaccio and Natalis Comes. We are dealing with more than specific borrowings. The important thing is Spenser's community of thought with them, which manifests itself in a common conception of the meaning and value of classic myth and of poetry in general. The result of this community of thought is a striking parallelism between classic myth as viewed allegorically by Comes and Boccaccio and the whole fable of *The Faerie Queene* as treated allegorically by Spenser. The mythographers and Spenser start with the same conception of poetry and end by speaking similar languages, which are, in both instances, allegorical myth. It is not surprising, then, that Spenser should have drawn heavily for purposes of moral allegory on classic myth which he found interpreted in ways so congenial to him. In a very real sense, his use of classic myth becomes an essential and organic part of his whole performance; the Mammon episode, the vision of the Graces on Mount Acidale, the classical voyage to the Bowre of Blis become quite as much a part of the whole story as the "fierce warres" of the knights of romance, or the purifications in the House of Holiness.

IV

There are some poets, Dante and Milton, for example, whose natural habit it is to make clear distinctions in their thinking. The sources of their ideas are usually definite, easily traceable, and their affiliations with earlier thinkers clear. Spenser is not one of these; he does not have the habit of making clear distinctions. Rather, his mind seems to have been of a kind which synthesizes without analyzing, which tends to break down distinctions and to fuse together things originally separate. Efforts to find in his work the characteristic ideas of Plato, or Lucretius, or Calvin, have this difficulty to meet; and it is dangerous to say that here he is fundamentally Lucretian, or there Calvinistic. The very fact that one can even consider three so different thinkers as influencing Spenser bears testimony to the eclectic quality of his work. He uses his philosophic sources, not in the spirit of a philosopher who would integrate his thought by an appeal to the thinkers of the past, but in the spirit of a poet who is seeking to "fill every rift of his subject with ore," to give dignity and scope to his narrative by gathering into it doctrine and idea as well as imagery and incident.

In this eclecticism, Spenser is at once typical of his age and true to his own temperament. For he seems to have been peculiarly susceptible, in an emotional and sensuous way, to abstract ideas. He felt them. Travelling in "this delightful land of Faery," he is "nigh ravisht with rare thoughts delight"; and he makes no distinction between these "rare thoughts" and the "sweet variety Of all that pleasant is to eare or eye." [53] He is the poet, first and last.

Thus Spenser tends to treat ideas as things, in and by themselves, and does not concern himself overmuch with the likenesses and differences between them. Hence his inconsistencies and the difficulty of relating him to a particular tradition of thought. Furthermore, his poetic temperament makes him change abstract

[53] F.Q. 6. Pr. 1.

ideas into concrete objects. Ideas assume physical form, are personified, take on characteristics which can be perceived by the senses and described. It is here that mythology plays an important part, for, in a number of cases, it supplies the material for such concretion. Mythological coloring becomes an index of the intensity with which Spenser feels an idea. Thus the Muses' lament over the sad state of learning and poetry rises to a climax when Ignorance is incarnated:

> Image of hellish horrour, Ignorance,
> Borne in the bosome of the black abysse,
> And fed with Furies milke, for sustenaunce
> Of his weak infancie, begot amisse
> By yawning Sloth on his owne mother Night. (*T.M.* 259–63)[54]

Two larger illustrations will serve better to show how Spenser mythologizes ideas and how his use of myth throws light on the eclectic, undiscriminating, fusing quality of his imagination.

Three passages in which Venus is the chief mythological figure are important to a study of Spenser's "philosophy."[55] In each, Venus is treated as symbolic of the ideas which Spenser is using. Do we find that she is a self-consistent symbol of a consistent body of doctrine? In the episode in the Temple of Venus, the central passage is one which translates the opening lines of the *De Rerum Natura*, giving in a nutshell the Lucretian doctrine of a universal generative principle which animates all physical nature.[56] Furthermore, Spenser describes Venus as of double sex, a traditional sign of her power over physical generation. His Venus is, then, Lucretian, earthly, materialistic. But in the same episode, Venus presides over a group of lovers who embody a central doctrine of Platonism[57] and the whole canto is conceived in terms of the medieval court of love tradition, which is certainly not Lucretian.

In the *Hymne of Beauty*, Spenser is following the doctrines of the Italian Neo-Platonists, and lines 25 through 56 present their

---

[54] Cf., further, *Aeternitie, Ate, Concord, Day, Fame, Giants, Hades, Jarre, Mutability.*
[55] *F.Q.* 3.6.29, f.; *F.Q.* 4.10.5, f.; *H.B.*
[56] *F.Q.* 4.10.44–47; see *Venus.*
[57] *F.Q.* 4.10.26.

characteristic idea that Venus stands for the divine Idea of Beauty, on the pattern of which God created the cosmos, and which is the source of all spiritual beauty in the world. Yet in the same poem Spenser again versifies Lucretius' opening lines[58] and says that Venus is the power which

> To the soule darts amorous desyre, . . .
> Therewith thou pointest thy sons poysned arrow (60–62).

Evidently, Venus is not just one thing. As a symbol, she is all-embracing, standing at once for physical and spiritual forces.

In the passage on the Garden of Adonis Spenser makes this still clearer. The philosophical parts of this canto present a material-istic, Lucretian conception of the origin of life.[59] But Venus is the presiding deity in the garden, and Spenser begins by telling us what Venus means. He says that, when Venus went out to look for her runaway Cupid, she

> left her heavenly hous,
> The house of goodly formes and faire aspects. (3.6.12)

Here she is certainly the Neo-Platonic Venus Urania, living in the World of Ideas, who appears in the *Hymne of Beauty*, a heavenly, spiritual power. But the same Venus brings Amoret to the Garden of Adonis, which is described as

> her joyous paradize,
> Wher most she wonnes, when she on earth does dwell. (3.6.29)

This is important, for it constitutes a mythological way of saying, first, that the Garden of Adonis is not the whole picture of life, but only of its physical, naturalistic side, and, second, that Venus re-presents more than a physical principle. She has an earthly house and a heavenly house. She is physical and spiritual, a symbol large enough to include within herself—taking all three passages to-gether—elements and ideas assembled from the Roman elegists,

---

[58] *H.B.* 15–16.
[59] Cf. E. Greenlaw, "Spenser and Lucretius," *SP*, 17.444–54. Prof. Greenlaw's arguments for Lucretian influence here and in *Mut.* have been questioned; cf. R. B. Levinson, "Spenser and Bruno", *PMLA*, 43. 675–81; Evelyn Albright, "Spenser's Cosmic Philosophy and his Religion," *PMLA*, 44. 715–59; Josephine Bennett, "Spenser's Garden of Adonis," *PMLA*, 47. 46–80.

from Lucretius, from Plato and Neo-Platonism, from medieval courtly love, and from the poet's own realization of fruitfulness and beauty, physical and spiritual, in the world and in human life. And this many-sidedness is possible because Spenser is using Venus as a mythological symbol. Without the mythology, such a synthesis would not have been achieved.

This same practice of assembling different and conflicting ideas under one mythical symbol is found also in the treatment of Cupid in the *Hymnes*. Much of the difficulty in interpreting these four poems arises from the tendency to regard them as philosophy rather than as mythology—as mythology used in the way we have just been discussing. For example, it is argued that the "Love" addressed at the beginning of the *Hymne of Heavenly Love* cannot be Cupid because in the *Hymne of Love* Cupid stands for sensual love, and the opening lines of the *Hymne of Heavenly Love* are about spiritual love.[60] To be sure, Spenser is aware of the difference between sensual and spiritual love; but this does not mean that he cannot be invoking the same mythical symbol in the *Hymne of Love* and when he says,

> Love, lift me up upon thy golden wings,
> From this base world unto thy heavens hight. (*H.H.L.* 1–2)

His conception of Cupid throughout the *Hymnes*, and elsewhere, is very elastic. In the *Hymne of Love* alone, Cupid is the Empedoclean Love which created an ordered world out of chaos;[61] he is the force by which all creatures "moved are To multiply the likenesse of their kynd,"[62] and the giver of that insight by which a man sees spiritual beauty in another.[63] He is the "imperious boy," with "empoysoned darts,"[64] and also the

> lord of truth and loialtie,
> Lifting himself out of the lowly dust
> On golden plumes up to the purest sky,
> Above the reach of loathly sinful lust, (*H.L.* 176–79)

---

[60] Cf. F. M. Padelford, "Spenser's *Fowre Hymnes: A Resurvey," SP*, 29.213–14.
[61] Cf. *H.L.* 74–91. [62] *H.L.* 99–100.
[63] Cf. *H.L.* 106–119. [64] *H.L.* 120–21.

words of which the address to Heavenly Love sounds like an echo.
As in the case of Venus, the symbol stands for the physical and the
spiritual, for the earthly and the heavenly, as represented by various and conflicting traditions. The mythological figure becomes a
receptacle in which differences do not distinguish. And it is significant that the mythological element in the *Hymnes* is almost
entirely Spenser's addition to his philosophic sources.[65] Where they
are abstract and metaphysical, he is concrete and figurative. He
sets out to write about Love and Beauty in terms of the philosophy
popular in his day, but he is really addressing the gods of his
imagination, clothed in the symbolism of classic myth, and expressing through that symbolism the many-sidedness of their
power.

What we have observed in his treatment of Venus and Cupid is
generally true throughout his poetry. He is seldom explicit and
single-minded. He is not preaching one rule to the exclusion of all
that might be inconsistent with it. His poetry is the fullest and
richest expression in English of the eclecticism which characterized
the Renaissance. His deliberate effort was to incorporate in his
great poem the best that had been thought and felt in the world,
before him, and by him. The result could hardly be straightforward
and simple and, given Spenser's particular temperament, it could
hardly have the kind of deep unity which Dante achieved, working
with a similar mass of tradition. What we get is something rich in
suggestiveness, "polyseme," to use Boccaccio's word again, a thing
of many facets and endless possibilities, in Spenser's own image, a
mirror, in which we may see

> What ever thing was in the world contayned,
> Betwixt the lowest earth and hevens hight.

Classic myth, as it came to Spenser, was "polyseme," rich in the
meanings and associations given it by generations of poets and commentators. Much of it was ready-made for his purposes; all of it

[65] For example, in *H.B.*, lines 43–53 and 57–61, which simply versify Neo-Platonic doctrine, seem
to follow Castiglione (cf. R. W. Lee, "Castiglione's Influence on Spenser's Early Hymns," *Phil.
Quarterly*, 7.65–77). Lines 54–56 and 62, which bring in the "Cyprian Queene" and her son, are
Sp.'s addition.

was plastic and adaptable. In many ways he made it serve his intentions: as poetic ornament for the high style; as a means of expressing a poetic response to nature; as a way of pointing out, through analogies and formal similes, the links of kinship between the people and actions of his created world and those of the world of classical antiquity. It provided him with abundant material for moral allegory and so became central to the most important avowed purpose of his work. It was a means whereby abstract ideas became intensely concrete, became persons who walk about his pages as characters in action. It furnished him with a body of symbols that could be used for feelings and intuitions for which no other terms would do. It was a language for his most personal emotions and aspirations. In all these ways it became organic and integral to his poetry, traditional and conventional to be sure, but also living and vital, because it expressed what was vital to him.

THE SOURCES OF SPENSER'S
CLASSICAL MYTHOLOGY

ACHERON 1.5.33.

Aen. 6.264,f. is behind the passage as a whole and accounts for the mention of Acheron: "Huic via, Tartarei quae fert Acherontis ad undas" (295). Cf. Hughes, pp. 372–77. N.C., 3.1, discusses the connection of Acheron with woe and wailing and twice calls its waters "insuavissima."

ACHILLES *V.G.* 526–30; *R.T.* 428–34; *Mui.* 63–4; 3.2.25; *H.L.* 233; cf. *S.C.* Mar. 97.

In the *V.G.* passage Sp.'s only substantial addition to *Culex* 323–5 is the statement that Achilles dragged Hector's body around Troy three times. For this he is probably indebted to *Aen.* 1.483–4 (S). Achilles' shield, made by Vulcan, is mentioned at *Mui.* 63–4; see *Vulcan.* Sp. has Artegal inherit Achilles' arms (3.2.25). There are other points at which he is associating Achilles and Artegal which help to explain this connection. At 5.5.12 he seems to be thinking of the story of Achilles and Penthesilea; cf. Gough, p. 225. Again the episode of Artegal's degradation (5.5.17,f.) may owe something to the story of Achilles disguised as a woman; cf. *Met.* 13.162,f. and Bocc. 12.52. The use of Achilles as an example of the power of love, *H.L.* 233, is based on *Symposium* 179E. *R.T.* 428–34 incorporates the oft-repeated story of Alexander at the tomb of Achilles which Sp. could have found in Cicero, *Pro Archia* 10; Petrarch, *In Vita* 135 (cf. E.K. on Oct. 65); Hoby, *Courtier*, ed. Everyman, p. 73; Du Bellay, *Déffense et Illustration*, ed. Séché, p. 134. At *SC.* Mar. 97 Sp. has Achilles' death in mind. His use of the myth here and E.K.'s gloss seem to follow Bocc. 12.52. Renwick, *S.C.*, p. 190, quotes Bocc. but omits the part which would determine the allegory of "lustfull love," expounded by E.K.: " . . . et ideo per talum non mersum in Styge invictam in Achille libidinem voluerunt."

ACIDALIA 4.5.5.; 6.10.6–9; *Epith.* 310.

The Acidalian Mount is introduced twice as the favorite haunt of Venus and the Graces (4.5.5; 6.10.6–9). Cf. Servius, *ad Aen.* 1.720: "Acidalia Venus dicitur vel quia inicit curas (cf. 6.10.8.6), quas Graeci ἀκιδας dicunt, vel certe a fonte Acidalio . . . in quo se Gratiae lavant." For the lovely extended description at 6.10.6, f., Sp. may have received some suggestions from *Met.* 5.388–91. On *Epith.* 310 see *Maia.* See also *Graces, Venus.*

ACONTIUS 2.7.55.

Reference is made here to the story treated by Ovid, *Her.* 20, 21. The apple in Ovid's story is not a gold one, but Ovid does make Acontius promise a golden image of the apple if he is successful in his suit (*Her.* 20.237–40), and, at *Her.* 21.123–4, Cydippe compares it with Atalanta's golden apples, which Sp. has just mentioned. Considering that he is here developing the subject of golden apples and assembling examples, these points may serve to explain his version of the myth.

ACTAEA 4.11.50. See *Nereids*.

ACTAEON 7.6.45.

Met. 3.173–259 is the basis for this brief allusion to Actaeon's story and is also the pattern for Sp.'s story of Faunus and Molanna (7.6.42–53). In this free adaptation, the chief resemblances to the Ovidian version are (a) the central episode, Diana revealed at her bath in a stream; (b) the reference to Faunus' horns (st. 47.7): while they are Faunus' natural possession, they may be meant to recall *Met.* 3.194, where Actaeon's first sign of change is the growth of horns; (c) Faunus, as punishment, is clad in a deer skin and hunted by the nymphs. Here Sp. differs from Ovid and may follow N.C., 6.24, who mentions as a variant version that Diana clad Actaeon in a deer skin and so had his hounds pursue him.

ADMETUS *V.G.* 425–7; 3.11.39.

V.G. refers to Admetus, without naming him, as the husband of Alcestis, whose life "she did prolong by changing fate for fate." Sp. is following *Culex* 263–4 fairly closely, his wording showing that he had before him a text which used Bembo's reading of line 264, "Ipsa suis fatis Admeti fata morata est."; cf. Plésent, p. 197; Emerson, p. 110. The reference to Apollo and Admetus at 3.11.39 is confusing and differs from classical versions of the story. Sp. seems to be following N.C. 4.10, perhaps a bit blindly: "Miserrimus factus [Apollo] operam suam Admeto Thessaliae regi pascendis armentis concessit." See *Isse*.

ADONIS 2.10.71; 3.1.34–38; 3.6.29,f.; *CCCHA* 804.

The story of Venus and Adonis told on the tapestry (3.1.34–38) shows points of similarity to Ovid's version, *Met.* 10.519,f., and also has in st. 38, as Upton noticed, a reminiscence of Bion's *Lament for Adonis* 7–9. The Bion passage and the most relevant parts of Ovid (*Met.* 10.535–44) are quoted by N.C., 5.16. N.C.'s Latin translation of Bion is closer to Sp. than is the Greek: "Dente femur niveo niveus iacet ictus Adonis." N.C. has all the material of Sp.'s passage, in Sp.'s order, except the metamorphosis into a flower, which is found at *Met.* 10.728,f. N.C. seems to be the main source for the passage. That Sp. knew Bion's poem directly and used it in Astrophel has been shown by R. Shafer in *MLN*, 28. 224–6.

N.C. has also contributed largely to Sp.'s most significant use of the Adonis myth, in the passage on the Garden of Adonis, 3.6.29,f. Considered mythologically,this passage shows two distinctive features. The "Garden of Adonis" is a real garden, an earthly paradise, not the little pot of quick-growing herbs so named in classical tradition (cf. Theocritus 15.113). Secondly, Adonis is conceived as "the father of all forms . . . that living gives to all." It has already been shown (Josephine Bennett, "Spenser's Garden of Adonis," *PMLA*, 47.46–80) that Sp.'s garden belongs to the tradition of the earthly paradise and that its name had been associated, vaguely and in a few places, with this tradition. It has not been noticed, however, that Sp. could have derived his two basic and distinctive features, mentioned above, from N.C.'s chapter on Adonis (*loc. cit.*). N.C. speaks of places associated with the worship of Adonis "in which seeds were sown and where there were many fruit-bearing trees, which were called the Gardens of Adonis, because Adonis delighted in such places." As regards Adonis himself, N.C. says that he is the author and nourisher of all seeds, who "gives nutriment to all things" and is called "of many forms." He goes on to identify him with the sun, which may be in Sp.'s mind, and interprets the boar as standing for winter, which will fit Sp.'s allegory.

The conception of the "Gardens of Adonis" in 2.10.71 and *CCCHA* 804 is fundamentally the same as that in the passage just discussed.

AEACUS *V.G.* 481–5.

Sp. is expanding *Culex* 297–8. *Met.* 13.25–6 supplies the information with which Sp. makes more explicit *Culex's* allusion to Aeacus as infernal judge.

AEGERIE 2.10.42.

A Fay who taught Numa, as Mertia taught Guitheline. The analogy is close and a natural one to the reader of *Fasti* 3.262 and 275–6 (S); cf. also *Met.* 15.479–90. At 2.10.39 Donwallo, as peacemaker and lawgiver, is called "Numa of Great Britany," probably with Ovid's passages in mind. This material from classic myth was not suggested by the English chronicles which Sp. is here following for his history; cf. Harper, pp. 93–4, 98–9.

AEGIDE *Mui.* 321; 3.9.22.

At *Mui.* 321 reference is made to Minerva's "Aegide shield." Sp. is here following *Met.* 6.78–9; but, for Ovid, the shield and the aegis are different things. Sp. is either revising independently or following N.C., 7.11, who thus identifies the shield with the aegis. The same passage in N.C. will explain the reference at 3.9.22 to Minerva's "Gorgonian shield": "Id caput [the Gorgon's] suo clypeo Pallas affixit et gestare consuevit." The form "aegide" is probably from *Met.* 6.79.

AEGINA 3.11.35.

The allusion is to one of Jove's amours. Like most of the others in this passage, it is taken directly from the similar list at *Met.* 6.103–114.

AENEAS *V.B.* 9; 3.9.40–43; *H.L.* 232.

At 3.9.40–43 Paridell summarizes the fortunes of Aeneas and the history of his descendants. Sp. imitates Vergil in introducing this sort of story at a banquet, and he follows him in some details. He uses "fatall errour" in the Vergilian sense (cf. *Aen.* 1.2) and again emphasizes the dominion of Fate at st. 52.5. St. 42.2 echoes *Aen.* 9.347–8 (Upton) and st. 42.6–7 alludes to the threats of Juno, *Aen.* 7.318. But Sp. omits the Dido episode and the descent into Hades and shows that he is interested in the story primarily as antecedent to English history. This shift of emphasis may be due in part to influence from Bocc., 6.53, who passes over the Dido episode in half a sentence, with a doubt as to its truth, and treats the rest as true history. In using the classical material as an introduction to Brutus and the founding of Britain, Sp. is following the English chroniclers, primarily Geoffrey of Monmouth, *Historia Regum Britanniae* 1.3; cf. Harper, pp. 168–9. Cf. also Hughes, pp. 333–38. *V.B.* 9, a reference to the combat of Aeneas and Turnus, translates *Songe* 9.5–8. Aeneas's *pietas* is interpreted as love at *H.L.* 232.

AEOLUS *Mui.* 419–20; 1.7.9; 3.4.10; 3.6.44; 3.8.21; 3.11.42; 4.9.23.

The genesis of Sp.'s conception of Aeolus is in *Aen.* 1.52–9. This passage, especially the description of the destructive power of the winds, seems to lie behind 4.9.23 and serves also to explain the passing references to the wind as "Aeolus blast" (*Mui.* 420; 3.6.44) and to the power of Aeolus over the "stormy enmity" of the winds (3.8.21). On Aeolus as father of Arne (3.11.42; 4.9.23) see *Arne;* on Aeolus as father of Orgoglio (1.7.9) see *Giants, Earth.*

AESCULAPIUS 1.5.36–44.

This passage as a whole, especially sts. 39, 40, owes much to *Aen.* 7.765–73. Sp.'s treatment of Aesculapius is peculiar only in representing him as condemned to endless punishment in Hades. In this Sp. was probably influenced by *Aen.* 7.773, "fulmine Phoebigenam Stygias detrusit ad undas," and he may have received a suggestion from N.C.'s remark, 4.11, that Pluto, when he found that Aesculapius was threatening to depopulate his kingdom through his powers of healing the dead, petitioned Jove "quod suum imperium Aesculapius exinanerit."

AESON *R.R.* 10. See *Argonautica.*

AETERNITIE 2.4.41.

"Aeternitie" is named as a divinity only in Bocc. 1.1, which appears to be the basis of the present passage. Bocc. says of her, "omne contineat aevum et contineatur a nullo," and quotes Claudian, *Stilicho* 2.424–30, which describes a mysterious, unnamed figure, "annorum squalida mater." The stanza as a whole, with its genealogy, seems to have Bocc.'s opening pages as a model. In Bocc., Aeternitie is the "socia" of Demogorgon, who is father of Herebus and Litigium and grandfather of Night. In Sp., Aeternitie is the parent of Herebus who with Night begat Phlegethon and Jarre (Litigium).

AGAMEMNON *V.G.* 545–92.

Throughout this passage Sp. follows *Culex* 334–57 fairly closely, deriving all his material from it. *Culex* 339–42, on the punishment of worldly vanity by envious Fortune, a congenial idea, he expands into a full stanza (553–60), with original addition in the last two lines. Other additions are at 564–6, 573, 588, and a fine expansion of *Culex* 349–53 in the description of the storm, 577–84.

AGAVE (1) 4.11.49. See *Nereids*.

AGAVE (2) *V.G.* 170–6; 5.8.47.

At *V.G.* 170–6 Sp. is translating freely from *Culex* 110–14, which gives all the material and is unique in speaking of the vengeance of King Nictileus (Bacchus). There is enough in the *V.G.* passage to explain the allusion at 5.8.47, although Sp. may well have known other treatments of the story of Pentheus and Agave and the Maenads, especially *Fasti* 4.457–9; *Met.* 3.701,f. He remembers the Maenads chiefly for their mad fury: according to Bocc. 5.25, they were called Bacchae "ob furorem potius quam ob virtutem."

AGDISTES 2.12.48. See *Genius*.

AGENOR 4.11.15. See *Founders of Nations*.

AGLAIA 6.10.22. See *Graces*.

AJAX *V.G.* 493–6, 513–25, 531.

Throughout *V.G.* 493–525 Sp. is following *Culex* 301–22. There is corruption in the text at *Culex* 319–20, for which Sp. gives his own version. *Culex* has here a baffling set of *alter's* which Sp. seems to take as continuing the combat of Ajax and Hector. "Th'one," *V.G.* 521, is Hector; "th'other," 523, is Ajax. Sp. defers reference to Achilles until line 526; cf. S.'s line references. The episode is based on *Il.* 15.696–746. *Culex* 325–6 refers rather cryptically to Ajax's death at the hands of Ulysses, but it seems doubtful whether Sp. caught the allusion. His original line 532 suggests rather the ambushment of Dolon, but this is inconsistent with the rest of the stanza.

ALBION 2.10.11; 4.11.16.

A giant and, at 4.11.16, one of the founders of nations, the most important one to Sp. He is following British chronicle history; cf. Harper, pp. 50–1. Bocc., 10.12 and 13.1, also mentions Hercules' victory over Albion in France.

ALCESTIS *V.G.* 425–7. See *Admetus*.

ALCIDES See *Hercules*.

ALCMENA *R.T.* 380; *M.H.T.* 1299; 3.11.33; *Epith.* 328.

At 3.11.33 she is mentioned in the list of Jove's amours. "Joying his love in likeness more entire" may allude to the fact that Jove appeared to her in the form of her husband, Amphitryon; cf. *Met.* 6.112, from which Sp. is working. The "three nights in one," instead of the more usual two is probably founded either on N.C. 6.1, "tres noctes in unam," or on Bocc. 13.1, who speaks of "tribus in unam iunctis lasciviendi spatium" and follows Lactantius, *ad Theb.* 9.424 in quoting from a now lost poem of Lucan: "Thebais Alcmene, qua dum frueretur Olympi rector Luciferum ter iusserat Hesperon esse." *Epith.* 328 and *M.H.T.* 1299 also refer to this night; cf. *Caduceus*. *R.T.* 380 simply mentions Alcmena as the mother of Hercules.

ALEBIUS 4.11.14. See *Sea-Gods*.

ALIMEDA 4.11.51. See *Nereids*.

AMALTHEA 7.7.41. See "Capricornus" under *Zodiac*.

AMAZONS 4.7.22; 4.11.21; 5.4.21,f.

The passage on Radigund's city of the Amazons (5.4.21,f.) represents Sp.'s most extensive use of the mythical warrior maids. They become an essential part of his narrative, even though he is using quite specific material from Diodorus 2.45 and 3.51 (see Gough, pp. 215–16), and from Ariosto, *O.F.* 20 (see Gough, pp. 207, 215). In the character of Radigund Sp. works more freely. She seems to combine memories of Penthesilea (cf. Gough, p. 225), Diodorus' Myrina, and Ariosto's Marfisa, all blended with his own ideas of the manly woman. On the story of Artegal's subjugation by Radigund cf. *Iole*. The passing reference at 4.7.22 to the swiftness of "the Thracian nymphs" probably means the Amazons; cf. *Aen.* 11.659–60.

AMBROSIA See *Nectar*.

AMMON 1.5.48.

Alexander "would as Ammon's son be magnified." Sp.'s use of Alexander here as a type of fallen pride points to influence from Bocc.'s version of the story, 13.71. Bocc. speaks of the "stultitia vetus" by which the famous ancients gloried in imagining themselves the sons of gods. Alexander spread the story that he was born of the union of Olympias with Jove in the form of a snake. "Not content with the multiplicity of titles which fortune, favoring his audacity, had added to his splendor, he sought by fraud to have Jove as his father and to this end suborned the priests of Libyan Ammon. O utterly foolish desire of that famous youth!"

AMPHION *R.R.* 25.

Sp. is translating *Ant. Rome* 25.5–8, which alludes to the usual classic story of Amphion and his part in the building of Thebes. He adds nothing which would prove further acquaintance with the myth.

AMPHITRITE 4.11.11; 4.11.49.

Sp. follows tradition in making Amphitrite the wife of Neptune; cf. *Theog.* 930. The lovely description of her at 4.11.11 seems to be original. Sp. is working out in poetic imagery his conception of the Nereids in general (cf. 4.11.48–53), of whom he knew her to be one (4.11.49). He may have in mind the identification of Amphitrite with water, made by N.C., 2.8.

AMPHITRYONID 7.7.36. See *Hercules*.

ANCHISES 3.9.41.

Anchises is here mentioned as the father of Aeneas and husband of Venus; cf *Aeneas*.

ANDROMEDA *R.T.* 649. See *Perseus.*

ANTAEUS 2.11.20,f.

In the story of Arthur's struggle with Maleger, leader of those who represent the temptations of the senses, Sp. has adapted the myth of Hercules and Antaeus. His use of the myth was probably influenced by the moral allegory which he found read into it by Bocc., 1.13, who follows Fulgentius 2.4, saying, "Fulgentius quidem moralem sensum fictioni subesse demonstrat, dicens Antaeum de Terra natum libidinem esse quae sola ex carne nascitur, qua tacta et si fessa sit in vires resurgit (cf. 2.11.42,45)."

ANTIOPA 3.11.35.

One in the list of Jove's amours. Sp. is following closely *Met.* 6.110–11.

AON 4.11.15. See *Founders of Nations.*

APOLLO

Apollo is son of Jove and Latona (*V.G.* 14; 2.12.13; 5.10.7; 6.2.25); see *Latona.* Sp. mentions several places associated with Apollo or sacred to him: at *V.G.* 19–24 (following *Culex* 13–17), Xanthus, "the woods of Astery," Parnassus, Castalia; at 6.2.25, Cynthus (cf. *Aen.* 4.143–9). See also *Pindus.* In Augustan poetry Apollo was thought of primarily as god of poetry, the inspirer and teacher of poets, often as a mere synonym for poetry itself; cf. Horace, *Odes* 4.6.29–30; *Ecl.* 3.62, 6.3–4; Ovid, *Ars Amat.* 2.493–6. It is this tradition that Sp. follows at *V.G.* 13–16 (translating *Culex* 11–13); *S.C.* Oct. 106; *R.R.* 32; *T.M.* 330, and 7.7.12, where he is "god of poets hight." Apollo's association with the Muses is a part of this. He was, for Sp., their father as well as their leader; see *Muses.* In the older mythology, Apollo was himself a singer and poet who entertained the gods with songs of their own deeds; cf. *Il.* 1.603. He so appears in Sp.: at 2.10.3 he is mentioned as having sung "the triumphs of Phlegrean Jove"; cf. *Theb.* 6.335–9 (Upton). He sang at the wedding of Peleus and Thetis (7.7.12); see *Peleus.* The idea of Apollo as scribe of the gods (7.5.35), for which no authority appears, may be taken as an extension of his office as a singer. The laurel is sacred to Apollo as poet and patron of poets (*V.G.* 672; cf. 1.1.19; 2.3.38; *Am.* 28); cf. *Met.* 1.557–67; Bocc. 7.29, who derives *laurus* from *laus.* Apollo is mentioned as god of prophecy as well as of poetry (2.9.48); cf. *Met.* 1.515–18, where these two powers are associated.

Apollo also appears as a lover, subject to the tyrannous power of Cupid. On 3.11.36–39 see *Daphne, Hyacinthus, Coronis, Phaethon, Isse.* 3.11.39.7–9, describing Apollo's changes, is rather close, as S. noted, to *Met.* 6.123–4. As god of medicine, "king of leeches," he appears at 1.5.43; 3.4.41; 4.6.1; 4.12.25. *Met.* 1.521–4 gives him this character and is especially close to 4.6.1. He is in the rôle of shepherd at 3.11.39; see *Admetus.*

It is as the sun-god, or as the sun itself, that Apollo, usually under the name of

Phoebus, appears most frequently in Sp. The chariot of the sun is mentioned at *S.C.* Jan. 73; *T.M.* 9; *V.G.* 67; 1.2.1; 1.2.29; 1.4.9; 1.5.44; 2.9.10; 3.8.51; 3.11.38; 5.3.19; 5.8.40; 6.3.29; *H.B.* 112. Cf. the description at *Met.* 2.107–10. When the sun is rising, the chariot and its steeds are usually described as "fiery"; when setting as "weary," with which cf. *Aen.* 11.913. The steeds of Phoebus are mentioned at *S.C.* July 18, Nov. 15; 1.1.32; 1.4.9; 1.11.31; 1.12.2; 5.8.40; *Daph.* 22–25. At 1.1.32 and 1.11.31 is the classical notion that the sun and his horses set in the ocean; cf. *Met.* 4.633–4. As the sun, Phoebus is "great father of generation . . . the author of life and light (3.6.9)" and his heat is "lifull" (*Epith.* 118). The direct source of 3.6.8–9 is *Met.* 1.416–37. The idea is paralleled in N.C. 4.10, "Hic est *generationis* et corruptionis unicus *auctor*." Perhaps one may regard this as an idea central to Sp.'s conception of Apollo in all his various aspects. See also *Laomedon, Liagore, Niobe, Phaethon*.

ARACHNE *Mui.* 256–352; 2.7.28; 2.12.77.

In *Mui.* 256–352 Sp. is adapting Ovid's story of the contest of Minerva and Arachne, *Met.* 6.1–145. The parallels were collected by S. and discussed by Reed Smith, "The Metamorphoses in *Muiopotmos*," *MLN*, 28.82–5. Sp.'s most significant change is the addition of the butterfly in Minerva's web. This causes Arachne to change into a spider from her own envy, whence the inborn hate of spiders for butterflies, of Aragnoll for Clarion. 2.7.28 and 2.12.77 are references to the spider's web by way of this myth.

ARGANTE 3.7.37,f., 47–51. See *Giants*.

ARGO *V.G.* 210; 2.12.44. See *Argonautica*.

ARGONAUTICA *R.R.* 10; *V.G.* 210, 397–400; 2.10.56; 2.12.44–45; 3.12.7; 4.1.23; 4.2.1; 4.10.27; 5.8.47; *Am.* 44.

Sp.'s early translations supply material on the sowing of the dragon's teeth (*R.R.* 10, translating *Ant. Rome* 10.1–4); on the Argo (*V.G.* 210, translating *Culex* 137–8), and on Medea's slaying her children (*V.G.* 397–400, translating *Culex* 248). Scattered allusions to the cycle occur in his original work: the episode of Hercules and Hylas (see *Hylas*); the civil strife of the Argonauts, calmed by Orpheus and his music (see *Orpheus*); Medea's murdering her brother (5.8.47). Sp.'s version of this last is closest to N.C., 6.7, who quotes *Tristia* 3.9,f., and says that she scattered the bones near the Pontic Sea. Hypsipyle is mentioned at 2.10.56, but nothing is said of her connection with the Argonauts. Sp.'s fullest use of the Argonautic myth is at 2.12.44–45, where an allusive summary is pictured in ivory over the entrance of Acrasia's bower. The material used here is classical and could be gathered from Ap.Rh., *passim; Met.* 7.1,f.; Horace, *Epodes* 5.61–66; Bocc. 13.26; N.C. 6.7. N.C. affords an explanation for the use of this myth in connection with Acrasia. In his moral interpretation, Jason's love for Medea (a kind of Circe, like Acrasia) is a giving in to "voluptatum desiderium"; he who was by nature wise and good was dominated by lust and "ad turpitudinem cupiditatibus moderatur."

ARGONAUTS 2.12.44; 4.1.23; 4.2.1; *Am.* 44. See *Argonautica.*

ARGUS *S.C.* July 154, Sept. 203, Oct. 32; 1.4.17; 3.9.7.

Sp.'s references are either to the living Argus who guarded Io (July 154, Sept. 203; 3.9.7), or to his eyes as they were transferred by Juno to the tail of her bird, the peacock (Oct. 32; 1.4.17). Both ideas were commonplace, then as now; cf. *Met.* 1.625-7. 722-3, and see Mustard, pp. 199-200, and E.K. on July 164. On 1.4.17 see *Juno.*

ARIADNE 6.10.13.

No authority appears for this stanza. Sp.'s substitution of Theseus and Ariadne for Pirithous and Hippodamia may result from a confused memory of the particular emphasis on Theseus' part in the battle at the wedding of Pirithous, as told by Ovid, *Met.* 12.210,f. and N.C. 7.4. On Ariadne's crown made a constellation, which classical writers usually associate with her marriage to Bacchus, Sp. may follow Ovid, *Met.* 8.177-82 and *Fasti* 3.507-16, who describes its beauty and, in the latter passage, says it is the crown which Vulcan gave to Venus; cf. 6.10.12-15 where Venus is in Sp.'s mind.

ARIES 5.Pr.5; 7.7.32. See *Zodiac.*

ARION 4.11.23; *Am.* 38.

At 4.11.23 Sp. is adapting Ovid's story, *Fasti* 2.79-118 (Upton), of Arion and his harp, by which he saved himself on a dolphin and calmed the raging seas. Ovid's murderous crew become pirates. The same myth is used at *Am.* 38 in a typical sonneteer's conceit.

ARNE 3.11.42; 4.9.23

At 3.11.42 Arne, Aeolus' daughter, is one of the loves of Neptune, to whom he came in the shape of a bull. Sp. is working from *Met.* 6.115-16, but Ovid's reference is cryptic; it is explained by Micyllus' note (Burmann 2.389), which Sp. may have seen: "Neptune made love to Aeolus' daughter, Arne, at which the father was enraged." The same sources will explain 4.9.23, which describes Aeolus' rage at the loss of his daughter.

ASOPUS 4.11.14 See *Sea-Gods.*

ASTERY (1) *Mui.* 113-144

A nymph transformed by jealous Venus into a butterfly. Sp. is creating new myth out of suggestions from the Cupid and Psyche story, to which he refers at *Mui.*

131–33; cf. *Psyche*. The chief connecting links are the theme of Venus' jealousy, the suggestion that Cupid helped Astery, as he helped Psyche, and the affinities of Psyche herself with butterflies. See Reed Smith, "The Metamorphoses in *Muiopotmos*," *MLN*, 28.82–85.

ASTERY (2) *V.G.* 20; 3.11.34.

Asteria is named among the amours of Jove at 3.11.34. Sp. is following *Met.* 6.108. At *V.G.* 20, "the woods of Astery" (*Culex* 15, "nemus Asteriae") are mentioned as among the haunts of Apollo. One cannot say whether Sp. knew the myth which connected Astery with this grove. It is told by Bocc., 4.21.

ASTRAEA *M.H.T.* 1–4; 5.1.5–11; 7.7.37; *Daph.* 218.

The immortal embodiment of Justice who lived on earth in the Golden Age, but returned to heaven and became the constellation Virgo, when human sin began to increase. See Gough's citations, pp. 168–9, and also Juvenal 6.19,f. and Hyginus, *P.A.* 2.25. All these classical references are scanty and allusive. The only formal and extended exposition of Astraea as Justice and of her life on earth is by N.C., 2.2. He says, the Golden Age was the age of perfect justice; laws were impressed in men's hearts, not in books. As human sin increased, Astraea fled the earth, but left behind her a volume of laws (cf. *Talus*).

Astraea as Virgo is most fully treated at 7.7.37. Here she is "a lovely mayd" whose lily hand is "crowned with ears of corn." This is not the more usual picture; Sp. may be following N.C.'s quotation (*l.c.*) from Manilius, "Spiciferae est Virgo Cereris."

ASTRAEUS 4.11.13. See *Sea-Gods*.

ASTYANAX 2.9.45. See *Hector*.

ATALANTA 2.7.54; *Am.* 77

In both passages her story is associated with the theme of golden apples, and in both her name is linked with that of Hercules. Sp. is following N.C. 7.7, "Not only Hercules was possessed of the apples of the Hesperides, for Atalanta too was captured by these apples. . . . It is told that Atalanta, daughter of Schoeneus, was ensnared by three apples of the Hesperides which Venus gave to Hippomenes." See *Hippomenes, Proserpina*.

ATE 2.7.55; 4.1.17,f.

The classical personification of Discord has become a real and active person in Sp.'s narrative, the companion of Duessa. She is an "old hag of hellish hue" (5.9.47), born of hellish brood and nursed by Furies (4.1.26; cf. 4.2.1), raised "from below Out of the dwellings of the damned sprights" (4.1.19). The description of her physical appearance (4.1.27–29) is apparently original, but may have received suggestions from *Theb.* 7.50 and Bocc., 1.3, who describes Litigium as "turpem et inhonestam faciem," and goes on to say that she is a force acting for the confusion of the elements, hostile to Concord (cf. 4.1.30). Cf. also, on Sp.'s possible use of Ariosto, Jones, *Spenser Handbook*, p. 243.

4.1.20,f. describes her dwelling and the symbols and trophies of her power which adorn it. Here Sp.'s starting point was probably *Aen.* 6.280–81, which would also serve to associate her with the Furies. The main sources of the passage are *Theb.* 7.40,f. and Chaucer, *Kn.T.* A 1977,f. (Upton). Comparison shows that Sp. had both of these before him and seems in addition to have drawn from Chaucer the device of using myth and history in sts. 22–23. The parallels may be indicated briefly: st. 20.5, "thornes and barren brakes"; cf. *Kn.T.* 1977–78, *Theb.* 7.40. St. 21, "ragged monuments"; cf. *Kn.T.* 1995,f., the paintings on the wall (from *Theb.* 7.47–53). St. 21.7–9; cf. *Theb.* 7.54. St. 24, "private persons"; cf. *Kn.T.* 1995–2030. On 2.7.55 see *Paris.* Cf. *Jarre.*

ATLAS *S.C.* May 142; *Ded. Son.* 9; 2.7.54; 3.1.57.

At May 142 and *Ded. Son.* 9, Atlas is represented, as traditionally, holding up "the wide compass of the firmament" on his shoulders. Cf. *Theog.* 517–20; *Met.* 2.296–97, 6.174–75; *Aen.* 4.481–82. E.K.'s euhemeristic interpretation of Atlas in the gloss to May 142 is found in Servius, *ad Aen.* 1.741, Bocc. 4.31, and N.C. 4.7. On 2.7.54 see *Hesperides;* on 3.1.57 see *Hyades.*

ATROPOS 4.2.48–49. See *Fates.*

AURORA *V.G.* 68–69; 1.2.7; 1.11.51; 2.3.1; 3.3.20; 3.10.1; 4.10.52; 5.10.16; 6.10.26; *Epith.* 75–76.

Sp. refers several times allusively to the myth of Aurora and Tithonus (1.2.7; 1.11.51; 3.3.20; *Epith.* 75–76); cf. *Aen.* 4.584–85, which is remembered at 1.2.7, where occurs also the familiar Homeric epithet, "rosie-fingered"; cf. *Il.* 1.477. Aurora is habitually given such epithets as "rosie" and "purple." Sp. would find an arsenal of these at *Met.* 2.112–15. 3.10.1.3–4 translates *Aen.* 4. 6–7 (Upton). Elsewhere Sp.'s references to the coming of Aurora, while in the classical manner, need not be assigned to specific sources.

AUTONOE 4.11.50. See *Nereids.*

AVERNUS 1.5.31.

Sp. is here remembering *Aen.* 6.236–42; but Vergil's lake and cave have been merged into the "yawning gulfe of deepe Avernus hole," belching smoke and sulphur. Sp. has been influenced by the medieval conception of hell and hell-mouth and perhaps also by Bocc., who, at 1.14, discusses *Aen. loc. cit.* at some length and identifies Avernus with Erebus and Tartarus.

BACCHUS *S.C.* Oct. 106; *T.M.* 461; *V.G.* 171–6; 1.6.15; 2.1.55; 3.1.51; 3.9.30; 3.11.43; 5.1.2; 5.8.47; *Epith.* 255.

In using Bacchus' name by metonymy for wine (Oct. 106; 1.6.15; 2.1.55; 3.1.51), Sp. follows classical usage; cf. *Aen.* 1.215; *Geo.* 4.102. On 3.1.51, "Lyaeus fatt," cf. *Met.* 4.11; Bocc. 5.25, where the name is given as one of the epithets of Bacchus; *Ciris* 229–30 and *Ecl.* 5.79, where Bacchus and Ceres are linked as here. In using "fatt," Sp. is apparently thinking of Silenus whom he does not distinguish as a separate person. At 2.1.55.6, the simplest meaning is 'when wine joins with water'; cf. *Nymphs*.

Bacchus and wine as inspirations of poetry (Oct. 106) are treated by Bocc. *loc. cit.:* "Poets also are wont to be crowned with the vine, because by their skill they are sacred to Bacchus"; and N.C. 5.13: "The heat of wine kindles genius." On *Epith.* 255 see Van Winkle, p. 110.

The conception of Bacchus as a champion of justice, like Hercules and Artegal (5.1.2) grows out of the classical tradition of his conquest of the east and his activity as peacemaker and fosterer of civilization; cf. *Met.* 4.20,f., 605,f., and Horace, *Epist.* 2.1.5–8. N.C. *loc. cit.*, p. 487, quotes the last passage and adds, "He was exalted as a god because of the many benefits which he brought to men, because of discords and contentions composed by him, because of cities founded and laws given." Sp. may be thinking of him in this capacity also at *T.M.* 461, where he is mentioned, again with Hercules, as one of those whom the muse, the "nurse of virtue," has glorified. See also *Agave 2*, *Philyra*.

BELLONA *S.C.* Oct. 114; *V.B.* 15; 4.1.14; 7.6.3; 7.6.32.

E.K.'s gloss on Oct. 114 identifies Bellona with Pallas. E.K. may have had in mind Bocc. 5.48 (Mustard), "Minerva was the inventor of war and is therefore called by some Bellona." Sp.'s own conception of Bellona is peculiar. At *V.B.* 15 he has apparently taken Du Bellay's "la sœur du grand Typhée" (*Songe* 15) to mean Bellona, which would make her one of the Titans. He has followed the French rather closely here in a description which has influenced 4.1.14 and 7.6.32. In the latter passage the conception of Bellona as a Titan, which is not found in classical tradition, may be explained as a memory of the early translation.

BELUS 4.11.15. See *Founders of Nations*.

BERECYNTHIAN GODDESS *R.R.* 6. See *Cybele*.

BIBLIS 3.2.41

An example of "such shamefull lusts . . . which depart from course of nature." *Met.* 9.454–665 tells the story of her unnatural love for her brother, Caunus. Bocc., 4.9., tells the story, following Ovid, and, like Sp., joins her with Pasiphae.

BISALTIS 3.11.41.

One of the loves of Neptune. Sp. is working freely from *Met*. 6.117.

BLATANT BEAST

The literary origins of the Blatant Beast were pointed out by Hughes in *MLR*, 13.267–75. However, it is not unlikely that the poet's conception was also influenced by some of the classical monsters with whom he connects the Blatant Beast genealogically. At 6.6.12, the Blatant Beast is made the offspring of Typhaon and Echidna, at 6.1.7–8, of Cerberus and Chimera. His points of resemblance with Cerberus are particularly to be noted. He is called a "hellish dog" (6.6.12). He barks (5.12.37), and has a hundred tongues (5.12.37), or a thousand (6.12.27); cf. Cerberus' "bloody flaming tong" (1.5.34). Cerberus was also born of Typhaon and Echidna (*Theog.* 311). In addition, Sp. may be using memories of Echidna as a serpent (*Theog.* 295,f.), and of Chimera, also an offspring of Typhaon and Echidna, as breathing fire (*Theog.* 319).

BOREAS *R.R.* 16, 26; *S.C.* Feb. 226; 1.2.33; 5.11.58.

The epithets and general characteristics which Sp. gives to Boreas ("bitter bleake," "bitter," "blustering," "wrathful") are in agreement with classical usage; cf. *Met*. 6.685–6; *Aen*. 3.687. Sp. is closer to Vergil than to Ovid. Ovid anthropomorphizes Boreas completely and tells of his love affair, playing with his character as a wind. Vergil and Sp. see him rather as a natural force, vaguely personified.

BRITOMART

For the name of his heroine, and for the association of her name with chastity, Sp. drew on a classical tradition. No specific influence of one source can be established; one can only point out the passages which would have been accessible to Sp. and would have helped him in his original creation. Diodorus, 5.76, says that she was a Cretan nymph, "a familiar of Diana," and sometimes confused with her. She appears as one of Diana's hunting nymphs in Claudian, *Stilicho* 3.251, 302–3. In *Ciris* 294–300, which Sp. used for his characterization of Glauce (cf. Todd 4.239–40; Hughes 348–54), she appears more fully in the same character. Bocc. names her as a wood nymph at 7.14, and at 9.35 gives a curious variation of the story which may well have stimulated Sp.'s imagination and perhaps have given him a suggestion for the warlike side of Britomart's character: "*Britona, Martis* filia, quae cum virgo adhaesisset Dianae, et perpetuo facto virginitatis toto."

BRONTES (BRONTEUS) 4.5.37; 4.11.13.

Sp.'s use of Brontes and Pyracmon in comparison with the giant Care (4.5.37) seems to derive from *Aen*. 8.425–8 (Upton), where Brontes, Steropes, and Pyracmon are forging thunderbolts for Jove in Vulcan's cave on Lipare. N.C., 9.8, quotes this and lists Brontes among the sons of Neptune, which will account for his presence among the sea-gods at 4.11.13.

BRUTUS 2.10.9–14; 2.10.36,37; 3.9.46–51; 4.11.38.

The possible sources of Sp.'s chronicle history, which finds in Brutus a connecting link with classic myth, are collected by Miss Harper. Brutus is descended from Assaracus (2.10.9); cf. Harper, p. 47. Sp. here combines material from the chronicles which trace his descent from Aeneas with his knowledge that Aeneas was descended from Assaracus (cf. *Geo.* 3.35). He wanted to trace the lineage back as far as possible. Brutus is the son of Sylvius (3.9.48); cf. Harper, p. 169; Bocc. 6.57. He finds Britain inhabited by brutish giants (2.10.7,f.); cf. Harper, pp. 42–4; Bocc. 6.57. These he conquers (2.10.9–13; 3.9.46–51); cf. Harper, pp. 47–50. He founds Troynovant, London (3.9.46–51); cf. Harper, p. 171. It is interesting to note that Brutus, like Aeneas, is driven to England by "fatall error" (2.10.9; cf. 3.9.41). This may be a conscious adaptation of Vergil.

CADMUS *V.G.* 171, 409; 2.9.45.

Cadmus, in the text of Sp., is little more than a name. The two *V.G.* passages are based closely on *Culex* 111 and 254, with Bembo's reading, "Cadmeio sanguine," in the latter (Emerson 110). The reference at 2.9.45 to Cadmus as builder of Thebes could be derived from *Theb.* 7.440–6, 11.180.

CADUCEUS *M.H.T.* 1292–99; 2.12.41; 4.3.42; 7.6.18.

The powers of Mercury's rod, as described at *M.H.T.* 1292–9; 2.12.41; 7.6.18 are from *Aen.* 4.242–6 (Riedner, p. 76); cf. *Od.* 5.47. 4.3.42 gives a detailed description of Cambina's "rod of peace" which, Sp. says, is very like Mercury's Caduceus. It is indeed Caduceus, transferred to Cambina. The immediate source of the description and of the allegory attached is N.C. 5.5, p. 434: "Caduceus illi dabatur cum anguibus geminis, mare at foemina scilicet, *mutuo connexu circumvolutis et concordibus quorum caudae demittebantur ad capulum caducei, qui concordiae securitatem significabant.*" Cf. also Servius, *ad Aen.* 4.242.

CAICUS 4.11.14. See *Sea-Gods*.

CALLIOPE See *Muses*.

CAMILLA 3.4.2.

Sp. is remembering *Aen.* 11.690. In the next stanza he compares Camilla with Britomart; and one can see certain general similarities between Britomart, who rides to adventures "only for honor and for high regard" (3.2.7), who has "puissance . . . for glorie of great valiaunce" (3.4.3.) and Vergil's "aspera virgo." Belphoebe also shows a trace of influence from Vergil's Camilla. Her "bow and quiver gay" and her "golden bauldricke" (2.3.29) seem to derive from the description of Camilla at *Aen.* 11.573–79, 648–54. Cf. Hughes, pp. 357–9.

CANCER 5.Pr.6; 7.7.35; *Epith.* 269. See *Zodiac.*

CAPRICORNUS 7.7.41. See *Zodiac.*

CASSIOPEIA 1.3.16.

In a passage which Sp. used for the Nereids, N.C., 8.6, p. 835, tells of Cassiopeia's arrogance in setting her own beauty above that of the nymphs, in punishment for which her daughter Andromeda was exposed to a sea monster, and she herself was placed among the stars.

CASTALIA *R.T.* 431; *T.M.* 57, 273; *V.G.* 23–4; *Daph.* 228.

From *V.G.* 23–4, which translates *Culex* 17, Sp. knew Castalia as sacred to Apollo and as a spring flowing from Parnassus. It so appears at *T.M.* 57. The phrase "speaking streames of pure Castalion" (*T.M.* 273) Jortin refers to *Silvae* 5.5.2, "Castalibus vocalibus undis." The allusion at *Daph.* 228 derives from the same conception. At *R.T.* 431, the "deaw of Castalie" is more definitely associated with poetic inspiration and poetic fame. Cf. Bocc. 10.27, which Sp. seems to have in mind throughout this passage (cf. *Pegasus*), ". . . cupidine famae atque temporalis gloriae a nonnullis affectio ponitur omnis, ex qua quotiens optatum consequitur, totiens fons Castalius, id est, abundans dicendi materia, oritur, quae quoniam Poetarum est, musis igitur dicitur consecratus hic fons."

CASTOR *R.T.* 386–9; 5.Pr.6; 7.7.34; *Proth.* 173–4.

All references are to the constellation Gemini; the myth of the mortal and immortal brothers is adapted to their character as stars. Especially with *R.T.* 386–9 cf. *Aen.* 6.121–2 and Servius on the same: Castor was mortal, but was saved by Pollux. "Quod ideo fingitur, quia horum stellae ita se habent ut occidente una oriatur altera." The idea at 5.Pr.6 that both are "twinnes of Jove," which contradicts the more common myth that Castor was son of Tyndarus, is supported by N.C. 8.9.

CELAENO 2.7.23.

The figure of Celaeno, chief of the Harpies, is taken from *Aen.* 3.245 (S). Bocc., 10.61, quotes Vergil and associates her with rapine and avarice, which may account for her presence just outside the cave of Mammon.

CENTAURS *V.G.* 41; *M.H.T.* 1124; 1.11.27; 2.9.50; 3.8.41; 3.11.43; 4.1.23; 6.10.13; 7.7.40.

Sp. mentions centaurs twice (*M.H.T.* 1124; 2.9.50) simply as "monstrous beasts," unconnected with any classic myth; cf. *Aen.* 6.285–6. The form of a centaur is one of the "dreadful shapes" assumed by Proteus while wooing Florimell (3.8.41); see *Proteus* and cf. *Erigone.* On 1.11.27 and 4.1.23 see *Hercules;* on *V.G.* 41; 4.1.23; 6.10.13 see *Lapiths;* on 3.11.43 and 7.7.40 see *Philyra.*

CEPHISSUS 1.11.30; 3.2.44.

At 1.11.30 Cephissus is mentioned as famous for its purifying waters. Thus Deucalion and Pyrrha, at *Met.* 1.369–72, sprinkle its water on them before going to the temple. On 3.2.44 see *Narcissus.*

CERBERUS *S.C.* Oct. 30; *V.G.* 345–52, 440; 1.5.34; 1.11.41; 4.10.58; 6.1.8; 6.12.35.

Sp.'s two descriptions of Cerberus are Vergilian. *V.G.* 345–52, a free paraphrase of *Culex* 220–22 (cf. Emerson, p. 107), is the most detailed and is the sort of thing that would impress Sp.'s imagination. He remembered it at 1.5.34, where there is also a reminiscence of *Aen.* 6.417–19; cf. Hughes, p. 310. Cerberus appears three times in connection with Orpheus (*V.G.* 440; *S.C.* Oct. 30; 4.10.48). A myth of the power of poetry over the law of death would be important to Sp. At 6.1.8 Cerberus and Chimaera are made the parents of the Blatant Beast. Although elsewhere (6.6.9) Typhaon and Echidna are its parents, the inconsistency is only one of detail, for Cerberus and Chimaera were themselves born of Typhaon and Echidna (*Theog.* 308,f.) and either pair, as hellish monsters of the Stygian fen, would serve Sp.'s purpose. Hercules' encounter with Cerberus is mentioned at 6.12.35. The closest parallel to Sp.'s version is *Met.* 7.410–15.

CERES *V.G.* 206–8; 3.1.51; *Daph.* 463.

V.G. 206–8 mentions the myth of Ceres and Triptolemus. Sp. is slightly expanding *Culex* 135–6. He might have known the story from *Met.* 5.642,f., N.C. 5.14, or Bocc. 8.4. Ceres' name is used by metonymy for bread at 3.1.51; cf. *Ciris* 230. *Daph.* 463 refers to "the mother of the gods" searching for her daughter, "Eurydice" (Proserpina); cf. Claudian, *R.P.* Ceres is a surprisingly unimportant figure in Sp.'s pantheon. Her place seems to have been taken by Venus and Nature.

CESTUS 4.5.3–6. See *Venus.*

CHAOS *R.R.* 19, 22; 3.6.36; 4.2.47; 4.9.23; 7.6.14; 7.6.26; *H.L.* 57–60.

In making Chaos the parent of Earth (7.6.26), Sp. follows *Theog.* 116. *R.R.* 22, with its idea of the seeds of things, "first bred . . . in great Chaos wombe," returning back to their original discord, is based closely on *Ant. Rome* 22.9–14 and should be taken into account in connection with the fuller development of the same ideas at 3.6.36 and *H.L.* 57,f. In these passages, using myth to express his theories of creation, he has adapted material from *Met.* 1.5,f.; *Symposium* 178; Ficino 1.3 (see Winst., *Hymns*, p. 45); Bocc., 1.2, who calls Chaos "omnium rerum creandarum immixta et confusa materia" and parallels Sp.'s use of "womb" with the phrase "ex Chaos praegnantis utero." Sp.'s Chaos is, in agreement with the Platonic rather than the Lucretian tradition, a huge body of formless matter in eternal strife and confusion. It still exists somewhere beyond the created world. For poetic purposes it is vaguely identified with Hades (4.2.47; cf. *Met.* 10.30; *Theog.* 814). For the association of Chaos with Daemogorgon in this passage, Sp. is probably dependent on

Bocc. 1.2, where Chaos is the "socia atque iam aeterna Daemogorgoni . . ."; cf. Osgood, *Milton*, p. 27. The ever-present threat of a return to chaos is remembered at 7.6.14 and serves to point the description of Aeolus' rage in the storm at 4.9.23.

CHARON *V.G.* 338–9.

The conventional idea of Charon charging fare and the rather unconventional idea that his ferry crosses Lethe are both supported by *Culex* 215–16, which Sp. is translating.

CHARYBDIS *V.G.* 542. See *Scylla*.

CHIMERA *V.G.* 19; 6.1.8.

At *V.G.* 19 Sp. is following *Culex* 14 in an allusion to Bellerephon's fight with the Chimera near Xanthus. At 6.1.8 Cerberus and Chimera are parents of the Blatant Beast; see *Blatant Beast* and *Cerberus*. The line "fell Chimera in her darkesome den" may be a reminiscence of *Aen.* 6.285–9, where Chimera is among the "multa variorum monstra ferorum" at the gate of Hades.

CHIRON 7.7.40. See *Philyra*.

CHLORIS *S.C.* April 122.

Sp.'s allusion to her gives no characterization; she is simply "the chiefest nymph of al" and, as goddess of flowers, appears appropriately in the April Eclogue. E.K.'s gloss, giving her story, is probably based on *Fasti* 5.195,f. (S). Renwick, *S.C.*, p. 193, also cites Bocc. 4.61, which parallels E.K.'s wording: "Nympham scilicet fuisse nomine Chlorin a Zephiro dilectam, et in coniugem acceptam, eique ab eo in munus amoris atque violatae pudicitiae omne ius in flores concessum." E.K. uses this same chapter in his gloss on March 16; see *Flora*.

CICONES *V.G.* 537.

Sp. is translating *Culex* 330. The ultimate source is *Od.* 9.39,f.

CIMMERIAM SHADES *V.G.* 370; *T.M.* 255–6.

At *V.G.* 370, which follows *Culex* 231–3 fairly closely, Cimmeriam shades are taken as a type of infernal darkness. At *T.M.* 255, which may derive from *V.G.*, "Cymerians dailie night" is made analogous with the intellectual darkness of the enemies of poetry. Bembo's note on the *Culex* passage says that, because of their habit of living in underground huts where no one could see the sun, Homer imagines them as "apud inferos" (*De Culice*, p. 100, quoted by Plésent, p. 175); cf. *Od.* 11.14–16.

CLIMENE 3.11.38

Mother of Phaethon by Apollo. See *Phaethon*.

CLIO See *Muses*.

CLOTHO 4.2.50; *H.L.* 63. See *Fates*.

COCYTUS 1.1.37; 2.7.56–57; 3.4.55.

"In which full many soules do endlesse wayle and weepe." (2.7.56.9). Cocytus as a river of wailing and weeping is traditional. For Bocc., 1.14, it symbolizes "luctus et lachrymae." N.C., 3.Pr., p. 185, says, "Cocytus . . . gravissimus et tristissimus amnis, cuius fremitus querularum animarum voces imitabatur," which might easily have suggested Sp.'s line. Cf. also *Aen.* 6.426, of the Styx, "Continuo auditae voces, vagitus et ingens." In Sp. the damned souls are represented as immersed in the flood. This conception is not common in classical tradition, but cf. Plato, *Phaedo* 113. The idea may come from Dante, *Inferno* 7.109, although Sp.'s use of Dante has not been proved unless we accept it here and in the case of Phlegethon.

CONCORD 4.10.31–36

Sp. may have derived suggestions for the scene he describes here from reading about the famous Roman Temple of Concord (cf. *Fasti* 1.637–50, 3.891–2, 6.637–48), but the passage is essentially original. Lady Concord is a mythical expression of the Neo-Platonic doctrine of the cosmic love which holds in harmony the four elements and all the conflicting forces of the world. In the figures of her two sons, Sp. makes realistic myth of the Empedoclean doctrine of Love and Hate. The original suggestion for the use of Lady Concord here may have come, as Lee suggests, from Ovid's phrase, "concordi pace ligavit," in a passage which is a source for the ideas she embodies (*Met.* 1.25,f.).

CORONIS 3.11.37.

One of the unlucky loves of Apollo. Sp. is following *Met.* 2.542–632 (S) for the story. Ovid, like Sp., emphasizes Apollo's grief. Nothing appears which would explain Sp.'s statement that Coronis was changed into a sweetbriar.

CORYBANTES 7.6.27. See *Cybele*.

CREUSA 2.12.45. See *Argonautica*.

CUPID

At all points except one (*H.L.* 50–56) Sp. follows the common classical tradition which makes Cupid the son of Venus. He varies, however, from the more common mythology in making Jove his father (*Mui.* 94; 1.Pr.3). S. cites *Ciris* 134, "pater et avus idem Iuppiter." Sp. might be following Bocc., 11.5, who speaks of Amor, son of Jove and Venus. At *CCCHA* 799–804, Cupid is born, "without syre," of Venus, "both male and female." S. cites Servius, *ad Aen.* 2.632; cf. also Macrobius, *Saturnalia* 3.8.1, and Bocc., 3.22, who follows Servius. At *H.L.* 50–56 Sp. mixes this myth of Cupid's birth with that of Plenty and Penury; see *Plenty*. In the same passage,

Cupid is called "a chyld . . . yet the eldest." Cf. *Symposium* 178, where he is called the eldest of the gods, following *Theog.* 116–120, and *Symposium* 195, where he is called the youngest. Ficino's attempted reconciliation of these two ideas (5.10, quoted by Winst., *Hymns*, p. 45) is probably behind Sp.'s lines.

One may distinguish three different aspects of Sp.'s Cupid, though sharp divisions between them do not hold. There is the conception of the great God of Love, "God of Might" (*H.L.* 43), "Lord of all the world" (*CCCHA* 883), a symbol of Love as a cosmic force which created the world out of Chaos (cf. *Theog.* 116–120), which maintains the order of its elements and inspires life and generation. *H.L.* 43,f. and *CCCHA* 835,f. present this conception most fully. Lee cites Ficino 3.2 (quoted by Winst., *Hymns*, p. lx) as the central source of these passages. The same ideas, more explicitly attached to the Cupid of classic myth, are found in N.C. 4.14, "Nihil aliud, ut dicebam, esse Cupidinem antiqui senserunt, nisi illud quod Empedocles vim similium divinam coire et coalescere cupientium: vel, ut melius dicam, mentem divinam quae has ipsas motiones ipsi naturae inducat."

More prominent is the conception of Cupid characteristic of Latin poetry and associated particularly with Alexandrianism. In this tradition he is the little boy, blind, winged, armed with bow and arrows,[1] capricious and cruel in his sporting with human hearts. The Alexandrian and Anacreontic elements are perhaps most distinct in *S.C.* March 61,f., an adaptation of Bion 4. Here Cupid is "the little god," with spotted wings, golden quiver, and silver bow. See E.K.'s gloss on March 79, on Cupid's "colours and furniture," and Renwick, *S.C.*, p. 189. Moschus 1 furnishes the basis for Sp.'s adaptation of the story of runaway Cupid at 3.6.11,f. More specifically Anacreontic are the *Epigrams*. *Epig.* 2 and 3 are free renderings of Marot, *Epigrammes* 64 and 103 (S). *Epig.* 4, the story of Cupid and the bee, is elaborated from Theocritus 19 (S), with perhaps some reference to *Anacreontea*, Ode 40. In Alexandrian literature, Cupid was often changed from one into many, or was given brothers, such as "Sport." So at *Mui.* 288; 4.10.42; *Am.* 16; *Epith.* 357–9. On 4.10.42, Upton cited Horace, *Odes* 1.2.33–34; cf. also *Odes* 1.19.1; 4.1.5; Catullus 3; Theocritus 7.117. On *Epith.* 357–8 cf. Van Winkle, p. 120. Cupid as the cruel god becomes conventional in the Petrarchan sonnet: *Am.* 10; cf. Petrarch 2,3. As the conventional symbol for the power of love he appears also at 2.3.23; 2.9.18; 2.9.34; 3.1.39; 3.2.35; 3.4.9; 4.Pr.5; 4.7.15; 6.10.1; *CCCHA* 766,f. 3.4.9, imagining Love as pilot of a ship is rather close to *Heroides* 15.215, "Ipse gubernabit residens in puppe Cupido."

In medieval love literature, Cupid retains his classical accoutrements, but he is no longer a little boy, but a great god, a king, sometimes almost a saint.[2] Thus in

---

[1] Sp.'s references to Cupid's wings, bow, and arrows may be collected from Whitman. *S.C.* March 96 and 3.11.47 should be added to his lists. The arrows of lead and gold (*Mui* 292; 3.11.36, 46; *CCCHA* 807; E.K. on March 79) go back to *Met.* 1.469–71, but come later to symbolize happy and unhappy love, as in Sp; cf. Chaucer, *Kn. Tale* A 1963–6; Gower, *Con. Am.* 3.1701–5; *The Court of Love* 1315–16; Marot, *Temple de Cupidon*; Sidney, *Arcadia*, song at 2.14.2. The arrows also come to symbolize the power of Love in the lady's eye: *Am.* 57; cf. Petrarch 21, 86.

[2] See W. A. Neilson, *The Origins and Sources of the "Court of Love,"* especially pp. 35–36, 78–9, 140, 147.

Sp. he is a tyrant (Oct. 98; 3.11; 3.12.22; 3.2.23; *H.L.* 134). He is a king (*Am.* 19; *H.L.* 305), "my liege lord" (*Mui.* 102). The lover is his "vassal" (*H.L.* 142).[3] This medieval Cupid is most in evidence in 3.11, and 12. Here he is "the Winged God," fierce, cruel, a victor rejoicing in his triumphs. There are several works which may have been models for these cantos. In Petrarch's *Trionfo d'Amore*, Cupid appears as a victorious war-lord, ruling over unhappy lovers who, as in Sp., are persons of classic myth. In the *Court of Love* (Skeat, *Chaucer* 7.409–447) there are, as in 3.11.30, f., pictorial representations of the power of love, drawn from myth, and, as in 3.12. 7,f., there are the personified abstractions conventional in dream-vision literature, attending on the god. Marot's *Temple de Cupidon* (*Œuvres*, ed. Jannet, 1.8–25) also has these personifications associated with Cupid and offers parallels to the description of the image of Cupid at 3.11. 47–48. Sp. would naturally turn to Chaucer. In *P.F.* 211,f., Cupid appears attended by the usual allegorical figures. In the *Prol. L.G.W.* B 226–40, he is described as "aungelicke," holding two arrows and looking sternly; cf. 3.12.22. The description of him at *Kn. Tale* A 1963–6 is very close to 3.11.48.1–2 (Upton). The other important appearance of the medieval god of love is at 6.7.32,f., where Cupid holds his court on St. Valentine's Day. Here again Sp. may have had *Prol. L.G.W.* in mind. The situation, the legal coloring, and the allegorical figures are also paralleled in the *Court of Love*. Cf. Fowler, *op. cit.*, pp. 103–6. The lost *Court of Cupid*, mentioned by E.K. in the prefatory letter to Harvey, if not used here, at least shows Sp.'s early interest in the tradition. We may class also as a part of the medieval conception the treatment of Scudamour as "Cupid's Man" (4.10.54), who bears the Shield of Love (3.11.7; 4.1.2, 39; 4.10.3,4.), and likewise, in a more general way, the association of Cupid with springtime (March 22; 7.7.34; *Am.* 4,7,19).

On 3.11.30,f. see *Apollo, Bacchus, Jove, Mars, Neptune, Saturn;* on 2.8.6 see *Ida;* on *H.L.* 57–63 see *Fates;* on *Mui.* 131 and 3.6.50–51 see *Psyche*.

CYBELE *R.R.* 6; 1.6.15; 4.11.28.

R.R. 6 follows *Ant. Rome* 6 closely, and that in turn imitates *Aen.* 6.784–87. Both *R.R.* and *Aen.* have probably influenced the description at 4.11.28. At 1.6.15 the "franticke rites" of the Corybantes in honor of Cybele are mentioned. S. cites *Fasti* 4.201,f., which recounts the origin of the custom. Cf. also Lucretius 2.618,f.; Strabo 469, 567. N.C., 9.5, says that the Corybantes in their rites imitate madness and fury and "are called Corybantes because they throw their heads about like madmen." Cf. 1.6.15.3.

CYCLOPS *V.G.* 541

This passing reference to the story of Polyphemus translates *Culex* 332. Sp. seems to have had Polyphemus in mind in the passage on the savage man, Lust, 4.7.5,f.; with 4.7.20.3–7 cf. *Od.* 9.240–3.

---

[3] See E. B. Fowler, *Spenser and the Courts of Love*, pp. 65, f.; W. G. Dodd, *Courtly Love in Chaucer and Gower*, pp. 18–20, the influence of feudalism on the medieval conception of Cupid.

CYMO 4.11.51. See *Nereids.*

CYMODOCE (CYMOENT) 3.4.19,f.; 4.11.50.

Of the fifty Nereids listed at 4.11.48–53, Cymodoce is the one whom Sp. has developed most and made his own. She steps out of classical literature into Sp.'s own story (3.4.19,f.), but at the same time remains the Nereid of myth. Her story has several features which seem to indicate that Sp. is reworking the story of Thetis (a Nereid) and Peleus and Achilles. Like Dumarin, Peleus caught Thetis asleep in her secret cave (*Met.* 11.217,f.). In both stories, the son born of this union was sheltered from the haps of life because of his mother's foreknowledge of some special danger that would be her son's undoing (cf. *Met.* 13.162,f.). In each case, this fate was the love of a woman. In Marinell's case, this is clearly understood and he escapes death. Following Bocc. 12.52 and N.C. 9.12, Sp. believed that Achilles met his death through love of Polyxena, which lured him into Troy, alone and unarmed, where he was shot in the heel by Paris (cf. *Achilles*). The destinies of Marinell and Achilles were thus, to Sp., similar. He is still adapting and recreating at 3.4.32–33, where he describes Cymodoce's chariot, drawn by dolphins over Neptune's "broad round back"; cf. *Aen.* 5.817–26, which describes the chariot of Neptune and mentions Cymodoce and Thetis; cf. also Moschus 2.110–23.

CYNTHIA See *Diana.*

CYNTHUS 2.3.31; 6.2.25; 7.7.50. See *Apollo, Diana.*

CYPARISSUS 1.6.17.

In associating Cyparissus with Silvanus, Sp. is probably following N.C. or Bocc. N.C., 5.10, says, "The story is that Cyparissus was loved by Silvanus, wherefore he was changed into the tree of the same name, and Silvanus is said always to carry a branch of it in his hands," and quotes *Geo.* 1.20. Bocc.'s account (13.17) has what may be verbal parallels to Sp.: "Sylvanus, sylvarum deus, [Cyparissum] amavit, qui, cum haberet *mansuetissimam cervam, eamque summe diligeret,* illam Sylvanus inadvertenter occidit, quamobrem Cyparissus summe dolens mortuus est, Sylvanus autem illum in arborem sui nominis vertit."

CYTHEREA *T.M.* 397; *Mui.* 98; 3.6.20; *H.B.* 260. See *Venus.*

CYTHERON 3.6.29; 6.10.9

In speaking of Mount Cytheron as the haunt of Venus where she keeps her principal court, Sp. differs from classical tradition and follows either Chaucer, *Kn. Tale* A 1936, 2223 (Todd 7.93) or Bocc. 3.22: "Cytherea is so called either from the island of Cythera or from Mount Cytheron, where especially she is wont to be worshipped."

DAEMOGORGON 1.1.37; 1.5.22; 4.2.47.

The history of this deity prior to Sp. can only be indicated. The starting-point is Plato's Δημιουργός (*Republic* 530A; *Timaeus* 40C). At *Theb.* 4.516, Tiresias invokes a mysterious deity, "triplicis mundi summum, quem scire nefastum." Lact.'s note on this line is crucial: "Dicit autem deum δημιουργόν" (so the Teubner text). On the name in question, two Mss. read "demoirgon;" two others read "demogorgon." It is the later form with which the poets have conjured. From a Ms. variant, it becomes in Bocc. (1.1) the name of the primal deity. He is "the greatest majesty of shadows," the grandfather of all the gods; he lives in the bowels of the earth, surrounded by cloud and vapor (cf. 4.2.47). He is the creator of all things. Caves are associated with him "apud rusticos" and people are afraid to utter his name. Citing Lucan 6.744, Bocc. identifies him with the "Gorgon" there invoked (cf. 1.1.37). Bocc.'s etymology of the name relates it to δαίμων and γεωργός: he is the daemon of the earth. Sp.'s conception of Daemogorgon is essentially the same as Bocc.'s. In addition, he shows more specific indebtedness in suggesting, by spelling, Bocc.'s etymology of the name, and in the identification, made by both, of Daemogorgon with Lucan's Gorgon.

DAMON and PYTHIAS 4.10.27.

Classical versions of the story give Phintias instead of Pythias; cf. Cicero, *De Officiis* 3.45; Valerius Maximus 4.7.ext.1. Sp. is following oral tradition, or perhaps such a conventional list of famous friends as that quoted from Lyly under *Orestes*.

DANAE 3.11.31.

Sp. is elaborating on *Met.* 6.113 and for nearly all the details of his elaboration he is clearly dependent on N.C. 7.18, p. 802: "He [Jove] is said to have flown down *from the roof* in the likeness of gold, which she took *into her lap*." Then, quoting Horace, *Odes* 3.16.1–8, "Inclusam Danaen *turris aënea* Robustaeque fores." The stanza thus incorporates material from Ovid, N.C., and Horace in N.C.'s quotation.

DANAIDS *V.G.* 393–6; 1.5.35.

V.G. 393–6, translating *Culex* 246–7, tells, without naming them, of the Danaids' ill-fated marriage rites. 1.5.35 alludes, again without name, to the more familiar myth of their punishment in Hades. The allusion is too general to warrant a definite source, but the suggestion for including the Danaids here may have come from *Met.* 4.462–3, where they appears in a similar environment in a similar episode, Juno's visit to Hades.

DAPHNE 2.12.52; 3.7.26; 3.11.36; 4.7.22; *Am.* 28.

Sp.'s version of the myth of Apollo and Daphne differs at several points from the classical one. At 3.11.36, the association with the love affairs of Mars and Venus seems to be an adaptation of *Met.* 4.169,f., where Venus takes revenge on Apollo for his spying by making him love Leucothoe, to his sorrow. For the variation on the classical story at *Am.* 28, Sp. may be partly indebted to Ronsard, *Astrée* xi. Sp. takes from Ronsard the analogy of the laurel and, through the obvious connection of the laurel with Daphne and of the laurel with pride (from Ronsard), shapes the

Daphne story to fit his own purpose. The reference at 2.12.52 is still more in the manner of the sonneteers. 3.7.26 and 4.7.22 allude to the swiftness of Daphne's flight. Sp. may have been particularly struck by Ovid's vivid description of this at *Met.* 1.525–30.

DAY 1.5.34; 3.4.59; 7.7.44; *Epith.* 99.

There are a few points at which Day appears as a mythological figure. At 1.5.34 Night is called the enemy of Day, and at 3.4.59 Truth is her daughter. The Hours are born of Day and Night (*Epith.* 99); see *Hours*. At 7.7.44 Day appears with Night in the procession of the seasons. The passage was probably suggested by *Met.* 2.23–30; cf. W. P. Cumming, "The Influence of Ovid's *Metamorphoses* on Spenser's 'Mutabilitie' Cantos," *SP*, 28.241–56.

DELOS 2.12.13. See *Latona*.

DEMON *R.R.* 27. See *Genius*.

DEMOPHOON *V.G.* 201–3.

Sp. has misunderstood *Culex* 131–2, "Posterius, cui Demophoon aeterna reliquit Perfidiam lamentanti mala;—perfide multis . . ." Sp. misses the allusion in "cui" to Phyllis and translates it "in which," thus making Demophoon the tree. *Heroides* 2, the most obvious source for information on this myth, is, like *Culex*, allusive and assumes an acquaintance with the story which Sp. does not seem to have had.

DESPITE See *Hades*.

DEUCALION 3.11.42; 5.Pr.2.

Sp. takes the story at 5.Pr.2 from *Met.* 1.395–416 (S). The way he associates the myth with the stoniness of men since the Golden Age may have been suggested by N.C., 8.17, who thus interprets the story of the creation of men from stones; "At cum rursus rudes homines et religionis cultusque deorum ignari nascerentur, dicti sunt lapides." Cf. also *Geo.* 1.61–63. On 3.11.42 see *Melantho*.

DIANA

On Diana's birth see *Latona*. From Delos, as her birthplace, she takes the epithet "Delian" (*V.G.* 170, translating *Culex* 110). Cynthus Hill, on Delos, gave her the name Cynthia (2.3.31; 7.7.50; E.K. on April 82). She appears often in her traditional character as a huntress, followed by her nymphs (1.12.7; 2.3.31; 3.6.17; 7.6.39); cf. *Aen.* 1.498,f.; *Met.* 2.441–2. She is called the "soveraine queene profest of woods and forrests" (7.6.38); cf. *Aen.* 9.405, "nemorum Latonia custos." 3.6.18 gives the fullest description of her in this character. Here she has her bow, painted quiver, buskins, golden locks, "lank loynes." *Met.* 3.163,f. (S) describes Diana's disrobing in terms quite similar to Sp.'s here. As first noticed by Upton, the simile on Diana at 2.3.31 follows *Aen.* 1.498–9 closely. Belphoebe, who is being described, has much in common with Diana. *Epig.* 2 is based on Marot, *Epigramme* 64, *De Diane* (S). Sp.'s fullest and most independent development of Diana as huntress, with her nymphs, is at 7.6.36,f.; cf. *Actaeon.* Along with this conception goes her association with chastity, prominent in classical tradition. This is explicit at 2.2.8 and is implicit in most of Sp.'s references to Diana and her nymphs; cf. *Nymphs.* As the virgin goddess of chastity, Cynthia was a conventional symbol for Queen Elizabeth (*CCCHA* 166); cf. Raleigh's *Cynthia,* Lyly's *Endymion.*

As goddess of the moon, Diana, or Cynthia, or Phoebe, appears frequently in Sp. and most fully at 7.6.8,f. Here Sp. is creating his own pageantry, but some of his material is classical. Cynthia is sitting on a "throne" drawn by two steeds, one black, one white. The chair, or chariot, could come from *Aen.* 10.215–16 or *Theb.* 1.338. The black and white steeds are found in Bocc. 4.16 and N.C. 3.17. The idea of the moon's changefulness (7.7.50) hardly needs a source, but here Sp. may have in mind *Met.* 15.196–8. The description of Cynthia as "pale and faynt, As when her face is stayned with magicke arts constraint" (1.7.34; cf. 7.6.16) recalls the association of Luna and Hecate with magic charms and incantations; cf. Theocritus 2; *Ecl.* 8.69; N.C. 3.17: "Hanc [Lunam] crediderunt antiqui e caelo magicis artibus deduci. Quippe cum antiquae veneficae mulieres putarentur solem lunamque abolere." *Epith.* 372–89, in which Cynthia is invoked as the goddess of childbirth, is imitated, as Dodge noticed (p. 717), from the *Anthologia Palatina* 5.122 (Teubner ed., vol. I, pp. 129–30); cf. also Van Winkle, pp. 121–22.

On *S.C.* July 63–4; *Epith.* 372–81 see *Endymion;* on 1.5.39; 5.8.43 see *Hippolytus;* on 2.13.13; 4.7.30; 5.10.7; *S.C.* April 82–90 see *Niobe;* on 7.7.39 see *Orion.*

DICE 5.9.32. See *Litae.*

DIOCLESIAN'S DAUGHTERS 2.10.8

This is material on the borderland between classic myth and English chronicle history. The possible sources are given by Miss Harper, p. 45.

DIOMEDES 5.8.31.

The "Thracian tyrant," slain by Hercules. Sp. may be following *Met.* 9.194–6, but is closer to Bocc. 13.1: "Diomedes, king of Thrace, whose custom it was to kill his guests and feed them to his animals, Hercules conquered and killed and to the same animals gave him to be devoured."

DISCORD 4.2.1. See *Ate, Jarre.*

DISDAIN 6.6.16; 6.7.27,f., 41–44. See *Giants.*

DODONIAN TREE *V.B.* 5

The oak at the oracle of Dodona, sacred to Jove, is here taken as a symbol of the Roman power. Sp. is entirely dependent on *Songe* 5.1–2.

DOLON *V.G.* 536

Sp. translates the very brief allusion at *Culex* 328, "victorque Dolonis," in a way that indicates acquaintance with the story. Cf. *Il.* 10.314,f.; *Met.* 13.241–6. Sp.'s original character, Dolon (5.6.19,f.), may be in part an extension from the Homeric spy, with some reference to the etymology of the name.

DORIS 4.11.48.

Daughter of Oceanus, wife of Nereus, mother of the Nereids. See *Nereids*.

DOTO 4.11.48. See *Nereids*.

DRYADS *V.G.* 178.

The line translates *Culex* 116. See *Nymphs*.

DRYOPE 1.6.15.

Sp. mentions her as one of the nymphs loved by Silvanus. In classic myth she was the wife of Faunus (*Aen.* 10.551, S). But Faunus was, roughly, the Latin equivalent for Pan, one of whose loves was Pholoe (*Silvae* 2.3.8–11), mentioned by Sp. in the same stanza as loved by Silvanus. The confusion, or transposition, may be explained as due to the fact that Pan, Faunus, and Silvanus were all wood-gods and their names were sometimes interchangeable.

DYNAMENE 4.11.49. See *Nereids*.

EARTH *R.R.* 12; 1.7.9; 2.11.45; 3.7.47; 3.11.22; 5.7.10; 7.6.20; 7.6.26; 7.7.8, 10; *Am.* 4.

Earth appears as mother of the Giants at *R.R.* 12; 3.11.22; 5.7.10; 7.6.20; cf. *Giants*. The idea at 7.6.20 that new Giants were born of the blood of the old, given life by the fruitful Earth, was suggested by *Met.* 1.156–62 (Jortin). The peculiar twist given to the same idea at 5.7.10 is from Plutarch, *De Iside* 6 (Gough, p. 250). The story at 3.7.47 of Typhoeus, who, through incest with his mother, Earth, begat Argante and Ollyphant, is original, but may have received a suggestion from *Geo.* 1.278, "partu Terra nefando." At 1.7.9 Earth and Aeolus are the parents of Orgoglio; cf. *Giants*. On 2.11.45 see *Antaeus*.

Earth in another character is equally prominent in Sp. She is the child of Chaos (cf. *Chaos*) and the grandmother of all the gods (7.6.26). Cf. Ap. Rh. 1.1092,f. and *Theb.* 8.303, the address to Terra, "O hominum divumque aeterna creatrix . . ." Bocc., 1.8, quotes this and identifies Earth with the "magna Mater," Cybele, Rhea, or Ops (cf. 7.7.26), the "rerum omnium creatrix." In the presence of the goddess Nature, Earth makes trees and flowers grow up "of her owne motion, Out of her fruitfull bosome." (7.7.8–10). Sp. is here using a convention which goes back to *Il.* 14.347 and *Theog.* 194. He may have in mind Lucretius 1.7–8 which he translated at 4.10.45.1–2, "tibi suavis daedala tellus Summittit flores." See *Nature*. The mythological conception of Earth as the fruitful mother appears again at *Am.* 4 and in the use of the phrase "mother Earth" at 2.11.42; 5.7.9; 5.12.23; *CCCHA* 226.

ECHIDNA 5.10.10; 5.11.23; 6.6.9–11.

6.6.9–11 gives the fullest description of Echidna, parent and prototype of hellish monsters. The material comes from *Theog.* 295,f. (S), but Sp. makes the impression more horrible by adding suggestions of his own personal feeling, the like of which are not in Hesiod. Sp.'s Echidna is the mother of the Blatant Beast, Orthrus, and Geryoneo's monster; see *Blatant Beast, Geryon, Sphinx.*

EIONE 4.11.50. See *Nereids.*

EIRENE 5.9.32. See *Litae.*

ELYSIUM *V.G.* 421–4; *R.T.* 332, f.; *S.C.* Nov. 179,f.; 4.10.23.

At *V.G.* 421–4 Sp.'s translation of *Culex* 260–62 is not accurate and gives a rather misleading idea of the "Elysian plaine"; cf. *Proserpina.* In accord with a tradition of the pastoral elegy, Sp.'s Elysium, as described in *S.C.* Nov. 179,f., is not only like Paradise (cf. E.K.'s gloss), but is hardly distinguishable from it. Cf. Boccaccio, *Eclogue* 14.102–3, 159, 162,f. and especially Sp.'s immediate model, Marot's *Complaincte de Madame Loyse de Savoye.* With 4.10.23 cf. *Aen.* 6.637,f. Sp. has in mind Vergil's home of the "magnanimi heroes" not only here in the Garden of Venus, but also in the Garden of Adonis (3.6.50) and in the "paradize of all delight and joyous happie rest" at *H.L.* 280,f. On *R.T.* 332,f. see *Linus.*

ENCELADUS 3.9.22.

This allusion to the fight of Minerva and Enceladus in the battle of the Giants is paralleled in Euripides, *Ion* 209,f., "Dost thou then perceive her who brandishes her Gorgonian shield against Enceladus?" The fight is mentioned by N.C., 6.21. The description of Enceladus as breathing fire, "like to a furnace redd," may be a reminiscence of *Aen.* 3.578–80. There is no authority for the mention of Haemus in connection with this myth. Sp. may be thinking of N.C., 6.22, who mentions Haemus in connection with Jove's fight with another giant, Typhoeus.

ENDYMION *S.C.* July 63–4; *Epith.* 378–81.

E.K.'s gloss on July 64 tells of Endymion's being laid asleep in a cave for thirty years that Cynthia might "enjoy his company." N.C., 4.8, and Bocc., 4.16, tell the story and the latter says that he slept for thirty years. *Epith.* 379–80 alludes to Endymion's winning Cynthia by bringing her a "fleece of wool." *Geo.* 3.391 tells this of Pan and Cynthia, but Sp. follows Servius who, in his note on that line, says, "mutat fabulam: nam non Pan sed Endymion amasse dicitur Lunam." Cf. also Castiglione, *Ecloga,* quoted by Van Winkle, p. 122.

EPHIALTES *V.G.* 375–6. See *Othos.*

ERATO (1) *T.M.* 361–420. See *Muses.*

ERATO (2) 4.11.49. See *Nereids.*

EREBUS *V.G.* 313–14; 2.4.41; 3.4.55.

At *V.G.* 313–14 Sp. is following *Culex* 202. He probably had before him Bembo's reading, "Erebo cit equos" (Plésent, p. 163, Emerson, p. 107). At 2.4.41 and 3.4.55 Erebus is personified as the husband of Night and the "foe of all the gods." In *Theog.* 123,f.; Cicero, *Nat. Deor.* 3.17; Hygin., *Fab.* praef.; N.C. 3.12, Erebus and Night are the parents of a numerous and terrible offspring; cf. *Night.*

ERIGONE 3.11.43.

In this stanza Sp. has made what is probably an accidental transposition. He is following *Met.* 6.125–6, "Liber ut Erigonen falsa decepta uva, Ut Saturnus equo geminum Chirona crearit." Sp. links Bacchus and Philyra (mother of Chiron), Saturn and Erigone. Neither myth was very common in classical literature and Sp. nowhere else mentions either lady by name.

ERINNYS *V.G.* 394; *R.R.* 24; 2.2.29.

Here Sp.'s early translations have supplied him with myth material which has influenced his later work. At *R.R.* 24 Sp. is translating *Ant. Rome* 24.5–6, "Quelle ardente Erinnys de ses rouges tenailles Vous pinsetoit les cœurs de rage envenimez?" Scudamour, affected by a similar passion, is tortured by the "rouges tenailles" in the House of Care (4.5.44). The *R.R.* passage would associate Erinnys with the Furies, as a symbol of discord. She so appears with her "hellish brond" at 2.2.29. In the same character, Erinnys lights the bridal torches for the Danaids, *V.G.* 394, translating *Culex* 246.

ERROR *T.M.* 257, 317. See *Ignorance.*

ERYX 4.11.14. See *Sea-Gods.*

ETEOCLES *V.G.* 409–16.

Sp. follows *Culex* 254–7, but expands considerably to emphasize the bloody contention of the two brothers, Eteocles and Polyneices, who were "blinde through ambition and with vengeance wood." With *Theb.* and perhaps Bocc.'s résumé of the story (2.73, 74) in mind, he is on familiar ground.

EUAGORE, EUARNE, EUCRATE, EUDORE, EULIMENE, EUNICE, EU-POMPE. 4.11.49–51. See *Nereids.*

EUNOMIE 5.9.32. See *Litae.*

EUPHOEMUS 4.11.14. See *Sea-Gods.*

EUPHROSYNE 6.10.22. See *Graces.*

EUROPA *Mui.* 277–96; 3.11.30; 5.Pr.5; 7.7.33.

Sp. twice (*Mui.* 277–96; 3.11.30) adapts and makes more vivid Ovid's picture of Europa and the bull (*Met.* 6.103–7; cf. also *Fasti* 5.607–14). The picture is fullest in the *Mui.* passage. His additions here may owe something to Moschus 2.120,f., where nymphs and Tritons accompany the bull over the sea and celebrate Jove's newest conquest. At 3.11.30 Sp. seems to remember one salient feature of his earlier description: Europa's trembling at the sea as she is being hurried across it. 5.Pr.5 and 7.7.33 allude to the same episode. For the identification of Europa's bull with Taurus Sp. had the authority of *Fasti* 5.617.

EUROTAS 2.3.31. See *Diana*.

EURYDICE *S.C.* Oct. 28; *R.T.* 391–2; *V.G.* 433–80; 4.10.58; *Daph.* 464; *Epith.* 16;

H.L. 235. See *Orpheus*. At *Daph.* 464 "Eurydice" is a mistake, either by Sp. or his printer, for "Proserpina."

EURYNOME 6.10.22.

Jove and Eurynome are parents of the Graces in *Theog.* 907. *Il.* 18.398 associates Thetis and Eurynome. This, if Sp. knew it, may have furnished a suggestion for connecting this love affair with the wedding of Peleus and Thetis.

EURYPULUS 4.11.14. See *Sea-Gods*.

EURYTION 5.10.10. See *Geryon*.

EUTERPE *T.M.* 235–300. See *Muses*.

FAME *S.C.* June 75; *R.T.* 421–4; 1.7.46; 1.10.59; 1.11.5; 2.3.38; 2.7.2; 2.8.13; 2.10.4; 3.2.8; 3.3.3; 4.2.32; *Am.* 84.

R.T. 421–4 gives the fullest characterization of Fame as a figure of myth. Sp. is probably working from *Aen.* 4.173,f. Bocc.'s comment on this passage (1.10) renders it closer to Sp.'s purpose: "Mox sese attolit (*sic*) in auras, id est, in ampliationem locutionis gentium evolat . . . inde se solo infert, hoc est, in vulgus et plebeios. Et tunc caput inter nubilia condit, cum se ad reges atque maiores effert." The phrase "flying Fame" occurs at *S.C.* June 75 and 1.7.46; cf. *Aen. loc. cit.*, and also 7.104, 11.139. On Fame's golden trumpet (2.7.2; 2.3.38; 3.3.3; *Am.* 84) cf. Chaucer, *H.F.* 3.482,f., 588. Sp.'s use of Fame, determined primarily by his ideals of heroic virtue and heroic poetry, differs vitally from the classical personification of Rumor. Sp. has taken over only the Vergilian imagery, probably under the influence of Bocc.'s interpretation.

FATES *S.C.* Nov. 148, 163; *R.T.* 17, 309; *T.M.* 15–16; 1.7.22; 3.3.25; 3.9.42; 4.2.47–52; 4.3.21; 4.7.15; 7.6.33; *Daph.* 16, 387.

The fullest picture of the Fates is at 4.2.47–52. Here, the association of the Fates with Daemogorgon and Chaos derives, probably, from Bocc. (1.5), who says that they were the daughters of Daemogorgon and were coeval with the beginnings of things. Similarly, N.C. (3.6) makes them the offspring of Chaos and speaks of their being received into his cave. Sp. says, at *H.L.* 63, that Love, when he rose out of "Venus lap" to create order and life out of Chaos, was awakened by Clotho. Cf. Bocc. *loc. cit.*: "Clotho interpretari *evocationem*, eo quod suum sit, iacto cuiuscumque rei semine, illud adeo in crementum trahere, ut aptum sit in lucem emergere." At 4.2.48 Sp. gives, with more elaboration than classical sources, the conventional picture of the three Fates spinning and cutting the threads of life; cf. *Met.* 8.452–4; Claudian, *R.P.* 1.48,f. Mention of the threads of destiny occurs also at *S.C.* Nov. 148; *R.T.* 181; 1.7.22; *Daph.* 16. At 4.2.51 is the common classical idea that the Fates dominate the gods and even Jove himself; cf. *Met.* 15.781–2, 807,f. Reference to the part played by the Fates in the course of human lives occurs rather often: *R.T.* 17, 181, 309; 1.7.22; 3.3.25; 3.9.42; 4.3.21; 4.7.15; 7.6.33; *Daph.* 387, and most elaborately at 4.2.47–52. In many of these passages, the Fates seem to be regarded as merely capricious or vengeful, but at 7.6.33 their decree stands for the divine order, here represented by the Olympians. It is so interpreted by Bocc., *loc. cit.*, citing Cicero and Boethius, "Fatum appello . . . ordinem, seriemque causarum." The invocation to the Fates at *Daph.* 16 may, as Warton suggested, be imitated from Chaucer, *Troilus* 1.6–14. In E.K.'s gloss on Nov. 148, the statement that the Fates were children of Erebus and Night may come from Cicero, *Nat. Deor.* 3.17, or N.C. 3.12, or Bocc. *loc. cit.*

FAUNS *S.C.* July 77; *V.G.* 145; *T.M.* 268; *V.B.* 10 (1st version); 1.6.7; 7.6.46, f.

At 7.6.50 it is indicated that Faunus is the father of "the wood-gods breed." By wood-gods, Sp. probably meant Pans, Sylvans, and Satyrs as well as Fauns. At *V.G.* 145 he translated "O Panes" (*Culex* 94) as "O fauns." E.K. glosses July 77, "Faunes and Sylvanes" as "of Poets feigned to be gods of the wood." Fauns and Satyrs are linked at *T.M.* 268 and 1.6.7. Fauns, Sylvans, and Nymphs haunt the region around the Medway (July 77). This lack of distinction was traditional. N.C. (5.9) makes Faunus the father of Fauns and Satyrs and Bocc. (8.13) more or less identifies Fauns and Pans. Cf. *Met.* 1.192–3, "Sunt, rustica numina, nymphae, faunique satyrique et monticolae silvani." Cf. also *Met.* 6.392–3 and *Aen.* 8.314. At 1.6.7, where Fauns and Satyrs are "dauncing in a rownd," in "rurall meriment," Sp. has fused classic myth and English folk-lore. In the same passage there may be, as Lemmi suggests (p. 275), some indebtedness to N.C.'s idea (10, p. 1033) that the Fauns and Sylvans watch over and protect workers in the fields and forests, "nam cum nihil in agris, vel in sylvis . . . non praesente ubique Deo committi liceret." In two passages the Fauns stand for forces antagonistic to beauty and learning. At *V.B.* 10 (1st version) "a naked rout of fauns" destroys the nymphs' resort. This passage, translating *Songe* 12, was probably the basis for *T.M.* 268 where a "ragged rout of fauns and satyrs" destroys the bower of the Muses. Something of the same idea is implicit in 1.6.7,f. Fauns, like Satyrs, might stand for brute and uncivilized animalism. Cf. *Satyrs*.

FAUNUS 2.2.7–9; 7.6.42,f.

In both passages Faunus is true to the character given him by Horace, *Odes* 3.18.1, "Faune, Nympharum fugientum amator." Sp.'s original myth of Faunus and the nymph of Diana (2.2.7–9) is probably based on the story of Alpheus and Arethusa, *Met.* 5.595–640 (Jortin). The association here of Faunus with fountains and river nymphs and Diana would pave the way for making Faunus the central figure of Sp.'s adaptation of the Actaeon myth at 7.6.42,f. See *Actaeon*.

FLORA *S.C.* March 16, May 31; 1.1.48; 1.4.17; 2.2.6; 2.12.50.

The Roman goddess of flowers and springtime appears as such at *S.C.* March 16, May 31; 1.4.17, and 2.2.6. But E.K.'s gloss on March 16 shows that strange things had been done to her. E.K.'s material is not from Tacitus, as he says it is, but originates in Lactantius, *Divinarum Institutionum Libri* 1.20.6, and is transcribed by Bocc., 4.61, whence E.K. probably took it (cf. C. C. Coulter in *MLN*, 35.55–56). The idea of Flora given there is also found in other Church Fathers, Minucius Felix 25.8 and Arnobius, *Adversus Gentes* 3.23. At 1.1.48 Flora crowns false Una with an ivy garland in the lustful dream which Archimago sends to the R.C.K. It seems probable that the conception of Flora found in E.K.'s gloss is in Sp.'s mind here.

FOLLY *T.M.* 212, 317. See *Ignorance*.

FORTUNE 1.8.43; 1.9.44; 2.9.8; 3.4.9; 5.10.20; *Daph.* 498.

Sp. speaks twice of Fortune's wheel (5.10.20; *Daph.* 498). At 3.4.9 Love and Fortune are imagined as the pilot and boatswain of Britomart's ship of life and both are called "bold and blinde." The wheel and the blindness are common in the tradition of Fortuna which originates in the classics; see H. R. Patch, *The Goddess Fortuna in Medieval Literature*, pp. 11–12, 38, 44, 150. N.C., 4.9, also calls Fortuna blind and, on the subject of her wheel, quotes Tibullus 1.5.70. 1.8.43 and 2.9.8 allude to the old ballad, "Fortune my foe." See *Mutability*.

FOUNDERS OF NATIONS 4.11.15–16.

Except for Inachus and Albion, whom Sp. also treats elsewhere, (see under these names), N.C., 2.8, pp. 165–6, affords all the material needed for these two stanzas: "Infinitus prope filiorum [Neptuni] est numerus (cf. 4.11.17.1–4) . . . Phoenicem habuit [Neptunus] e Libya, et Belum et Agenorem . . . Aonem, a quo vocata est Aonia regio . . . Phaeacem, a quo Phaeacia dicebatur . . . Phoenicem, a quo Phoenicia . . . Ogygum . . . Albion . . . Pelasgus." Although S. implies that Sp. sought through widely scattered sources, it seems more probable that here, as with his lists of the Nereids and Sea-Gods, he took his start from N.C.'s passage which is the only place where he would find these names assembled in such a list.

FURIES *S.C.* Nov. 164; *T.M.* 45, 261; *V.G.* 394, 422–3; *M.H.T.* 1294; *R.R.* 24; 1.3.36; 1.5.31; 1.6.47; 1.7.13; 1.9.24; 2.2.20; 2.5.37; 2.12.41; 3.11.1; 4.1.26; 4.2.1; 4.6.17; 5.11.23; *Am.* 85.

Except for 1.3.36, where there may be a trace of the Greek conception of the Furies or Eumenides as personifications of conscience, the character of the Furies in Sp. is that indicated by E.K. (gloss on Nov. 164), "the authors of all evil and mischief." Support is given this by such passages as *Aen.* 6.280–81, 7.324–6, and *Ant. Rome* 24, translated at *R.R.* 24. They are the authors of discord. Thus Ate was nursed in hell by a Fury (4.1.26) and Discord is a firebrand of hell first kindled by a thousand furies (4.2.1); cf. the firebrand of Tisiphone (*Met.* 4.481–5), who brings with her Grief, Terror, Dread, and Madness. The firebrand of the Furies is carried over into the description of the non-classical "Fury" in the mask of Cupid, 3.12.16–17. Similar in spirit is the idea that Jealousy was nursed by a Fury (3.11.1) and that Ignorance was fed with Fury's milk (*T.M.* 261). Slighter references to them in the same character are at 1.6.47; 2.5.37; 2.6.49; 4.6.17; *T.M.* 45. Sp. shows a tendency to multiply the number of the Furies (1.7.13; 2.2.30) and to use them as equivalent to hellish fiends in general (*T.M.* 45; 2.5.37; 4.6.17; 5.11.23). On the Furies' snaky locks (*Am.* 85) cf. *Aen.* 7.445–8; *Theb.* 12.647. The idea that the Furies are in chains (1.5.31; 1.9.24) seems to be original, though Sp. may have got a suggestion for it from *Aen.* 6.555–8.

At *T.M.* 164 and in E.K.'s gloss on Nov. 164 Persephone is named as a Fury in place of Tisiphone, who appears only at *V.G.* 342, which translates *Culex* 218. At *V.G.* 422–4, translating *Culex* 261, "grim Persephone" is urging on "her fellow Furies." A Ms. variant at this point in *Culex* gives Tisiphone for Persephone (Plésent, p. 79). Sp. may have found both names in his text and so thought that they applied to the same person. Given this notion of Persephone at *V.G.* 422–4, the substitution of her for Tisiphone elsewhere was easy. Cf. *Proserpina.* On *M.H.T.* 1294 and 2.12.41 see *Caduceus.*

GALATHEA, GALENE 4.11.48, 49. See *Nereids.*

GANYMEDE 3.11.34; 3.12.7.

The picture at 3.11.34 of Ganymede being snatched away by the eagle was probably suggested by *Aen.* 5.254–7; cf. also *Theb.* 1.548–51. When he says that Jove himself in the form of his eagle stole Ganymede, Sp. seems to follow N.C. 9.13: "Alii tradiderunt Iovem in aquilam versum ad ipsum Ganymedum convolasse et illum in coelum asportasse." He may be using N.C. *loc. cit.* also at 3.12.7, where the description of Ganymede and his peerless beauty is rather close to *Il.* 20.232–5, which N.C. quotes.

GENIUS *R.T.* 19; *R.R.* 27; 2.12.47–49; 3.6.31–32; *Epith.* 398–403.

The early history of Genius as a god of generation, the tradition of the good and the evil genius and its connections with angels and demons, has been fully discussed.[4] Only Sp.'s definite points of contact with this tradition need be treated here. As first pointed out by Warton (Todd 4.207), the main source for the description of Genius at 2.12.47–49 is N.C. 4.3, whose account of Genius tells of his "care of life and generation all," his guidance of man's life by means of "phantoms," his name, Agdistes; of the evil genii or daemons opposed to him, who mislead men with false and "guileful semblants" which draw them into lust and incontinence; of Agdistes' being worshipped with flowers and wine in bowls.[5] N.C. does not supply Sp.'s idea that this Genius is "our selfe," unless it is to be inferred from his statement that he is born with us. A closer parallel to this is in Apuleius, *De Deo Socratis* 15, "Animus humanus etiam nunc in corpore situs δαίμων nuncupatur. . . . Igitur et bona cupido animi bonus deus est. . . . (Identifies the Greek δαίμων with the Latin *genius*) . . . Is deus, *qui est animus sui cuique*, . . ." In using Genius here as "Pleasure's porter," Sp. may have in mind N.C.'s statement that the evil genius leads men into lust, and perhaps also Servius, *ad Geo.* 1.302, "Nam quotiens voluptati operam damus, indulgere dicimur genio . . ."

Genius, as god of birth and generation, appears at 3.6.32 and *Epith.* 398–9. On the former passage Warton quoted a passage from Cebes, *Tabula* (ed. Jerram,p. 3), which is a fairly close parallel. Sp. may also have been influenced here by *Aen.* 6.743 and Servius' note thereon. Vergil is treating the same subject as Sp., the destiny of souls in the other world, between incarnations. "Quisque suos patimur Manes." Servius renders this somewhat closer to Sp.: "Cum nascimur, duos genios sortimur: unus est qui hortatur ad bona, alter qui depravit ad mala (cf. 3.6.31.9). Quibus adsistentibus post mortem aut adserimur in meliorem vitam, aut condemnamur in deteriorem, . . . ergo 'manes' genios dicit, quos cum vita sortimur." Servius is probably following *Phaedo* 107D, which Sp. may also have in mind here. At *Epith.* 398–9 Genius is invoked in the poet's prayer for children. In using the words "gentle" and "geniall," Sp. is playing on the etymology of the god's name. On the phrase "geniall bed" cf. Van Winkle, p. 124.

There were Genii, not only of human beings, but of plants, animals, and places as well. The idea of the "genius loci" (cf. *Aen.* 5.95, 7.136) lies behind the "Roman Daemon" (*R.R.* 27, translating *Ant. Rome* 27.12–14) and the "ancient genius of that city brent" (*R.T.* 19).

[4] See E. C. Knowlton in *MLN*, 39.89–95; *SP*, 25.439–56; *Classical Philology*, 15.380–84.

[5] N.C. 4.3: "Dictus est autem Genius, ut placuit Latinis, a gignendo vel quia nobiscum gignatur, vel quia illi *procreandorum cura* divinitus commissa putaretur (cf. st. 47.2–4). His creditur . . . universam vitam nostram gubernare. . . . Nam existimatur Genii daemones rerum, quas voluerint nobis persuadere, *spectra et imagines* sibi tanquam in speculo imprimere, quod illis facillimum sit (cf. st. 47.5–7). . . . Figura quidem humana, . . . quem *Agdisten* appellarunt (cf. st. 48.1–2). . . . At si quis posthabita ratione *malorum spectrorum* et visorum ductu feratur, ille in multos errores incurrat necesse est, si spectra praecipue *a malignis daemonibus* oblata (cf. st. 48.3–6). Ita multi fiunt supra modum *libidinosi* . . . " When sacrifices were made to Agdistes, "*flores* complures humi spargebantur (cf. st. 49.1–2), *vinumque* illi in pateris offerebatur (cf. st. 49.2–4), ut innuit Horatius in secundo Epistolarum (2.2.143), 'Floribus et vino Genium memorem,' . . . " I have rearranged this slightly to fit the sequence in Sp. On the worship of Agdistes see also Strabo 469, 567.

GERYON 5.10.9–10.

In his use of Geryon here to cloak historical allegory, Sp. may have been helped by Servius, *ad Aen.* 7.662, where Geryon's triple form is said to signify the three islands over which he ruled (in Sp., the three parts of the Spanish dominions). For a good share of the descriptive material in this passage, he is indebted to N.C. 6.1, p. 677: "Postea vero iussit Eurystheus ut *puniceos Geryonis Hispaniae regis boves qui hospites vorarent* ad se adduceret. . . . Dicitur Geryon . . . *triplex corporis habuisse, canemque duorum capitum,* . . . *ex Typhone et Echidna genitum.* . . . Habuit vero suae crudelitatis ministrum *impigrum atque diligentem Eurytionem.*" Geryoneo, an example of Sp.'s habit of independently multiplying mythical figures, shares the characteristics of his father. His dragon (5.11.23) was probably suggested by N.C., *loc. cit.*, who says that Geryon also had a dragon, born of Typhaon and Echidna. For the image of Geryon (5.10.13), Sp. may have received a suggestion from Bocc., 1.21, where, referring to Dante, he describes an image of Fraud, with the face of a man and the body of a serpent, ending in a scorpion's tail, the name of which was Geryon.

GIANTS *V.G.* 40; *R.R.* 4, 11, 12, 17; 2.10.3; 3.7.47; 3.9.22; 3.11.22; 5.1.9; 5.7.10–11; 5.12.15; 6.7.41.

Sp. frequently confuses Giants and Titans and sometimes treats the names synonymously. Together, they stand, generally, for insolent and foolhardy pride and rebellion against established order; cf. *Titans.* He also tends to confuse the two battles of the Giants and of the Titans against the Olympians. To such a battle, on "the Phlegrean plaine," he refers three times. *V.G.* 39–40 and 5.7.10 may both be referred to *Culex* 27–8, or to such allusions as those at *Met.* 10.151 and *Theb.* 10.909. 2.10.3 tells of Apollo's song about the battle; cf. *Met.* 10.149–51, where the same matter and circumstances are found. Cf. also *R.R.* 4; 3.7.47; 3.11.22; 5.1.9; 7.6.2.

The description of Disdain at 6.7.41 may serve as a type for Sp.'s idea of the physical nature of the Giants. Characteristically, he creates new Giants of his own, born of the old. While one cannot cite definite sources for such cases, it is quite possible that he was influenced in a general way by N.C.'s saying (6.20), "Cum hi [Titanes] adversus Iovem pugnantes vulnerati fuissent, dicuntur ex illorum sanguine qui in terram defluxit, varia viperarum genera letiferorumque serpentum esse exorta." Something on these new Giants may be noted here: Care, the giant blacksmith (4.5.32,f.) who resembles Vulcan; cf. *Brontes*; Disdain (6.6.16; 6.7.27, 39,f.; 6.8.1,f.) seems to be developed chiefly from the idea of Pride, inherent in Sp.'s conception of Giants in general; Ollyphant (3.7.47–49; 3.11.3–6) is linked with classic myth only by his descent from Typhoeus and Earth; cf. *Earth*. Orgoglio (1.7.9; 1.7.14–18; 1.8.1–24; 6.7.41): Sp. here makes skillful and significant use of the possibilities of genealogy (1.7.9). Orgoglio is an embodiment of the combined characteristics of his parents, as Sp. conceived them. Cf. Hygin., *Fab.* Praef., "ex Aethere et Terra . . . Superbia" (Upton). Pollente (5.2.4,f.) may have some affinity with the classical giant Pallans, whom N.C. mentions, 6.21. Argante (3.7.37–54): She is substantially original, but Sp. may have taken the name and the idea of making her a giantess from Bocc. 4.16, where Argente is mentioned, as an alternative name for Luna, daughter of Hyperion. See also *Albion, Atlas, Brontes, Enceladus, Ephialtes, Orion, Othos, Pyracmon, Tityus, Typhaon, Typhoeus.*

GLAUCE, GLAUCONOME 4.11.48, 50. See *Nereids.*

GLAUCUS 4.11.13. See *Sea-Gods.*

GOLDEN AGE 5.Pr.2. See *Saturn.*

GOLDEN CHAIN 1.5.25; 2.7.46; 4.1.30; 7.6.14; *H.L.* 89.

Il. 8.18–27 is the *locus classicus* on the golden chain suspended from heaven. In making it a symbol of covetous ambition (2.7.46), Sp. has probably been influenced by N.C., 2.4 (cf. Lemmi, p. 277), who says, "Quod attinet ad auream cathenam, quod omnes Dii Iovem de caelo detrahere non possent, ego modo *avaritiam*, modo *ambitionem* esse auream cathenam crediderim." Writers after Homer also made it a symbol of the cosmic force which holds the universe in order. Cf. Plato, *Thaeatetus* 153D; Boethius, *De Cons. Phil.* 2, metre 8; Chaucer, *Troilus* 3.1744 and *Kn. Tale* A 2987–93; *Romance of the Rose* 16988–9; N.C. *loc. cit.*: ". . . auream cathenam, quae est vis aethereorum et superorum corporum inter se divinitus connexorum." In Sp. it is the "chayne of strong necessity" (1.5.25); Chaos is bound by a chain (7.6.14); it appears as the "golden chain of Concord" (3.1.12; 4.1.30) and as the chain of Love (*H.L.* 89).

GOLDEN FLEECE *V.G.* 211; *R.R.* 10; 2.12.44; 4.1.23; *Am.* 44. See *Argonautica.*

GORGON 1.1.37; 3.9.22; 4.11.13.

On 1.1.37 see *Daemogorgon;* on 3.9.22 see *Aegide;* on 4.11.13 see *Medusa.*

GRACES *S.C.* April 109, June 25; *T.M.* 180, 403; *Ded. Son.* 5; 1.1.48; 2.3.25; 2.8.6; 3.6.2; 4.5.5.; 6.10.9,f.; *Am.* 40; *Epith.* 103–9, 257–8; *H.B.* 254.

Sp.'s most extended and significant use of the Graces is at 6.10.9,f. He is elaborating on the traditional conception of the Graces as the handmaids of Venus, who delight in dancing (cf. *S.C.* April 109–12; *Epith.* 257) and in "play and sport" on Mount Acidale. Cf. *Acidalia.* The Graces are "daughters of delight" (st. 15). N.C., 4.15, says that they stand for "hilaritas et laetitia" and are "laetitiae matres." Sp. follows *Theog.* 907–11 in making them the daughters of Jove and Eurynome, "the fair-cheeked Graces, Aglaia, and Euphrosyne, and lovely Thalia, from whose eyes as they looked flowed love which looseth the limbs." St. 24, with its interpretation of their nakedness, is quite close to Servius, *ad Aen.* 1.720, "Ideo autem nudae sunt, quod gratiae *sine fuco* esse debent, ideo connexae quia insolubilis esse gratias decet . . . Quod vero *una aversa* pingitur, *duae nos respicientes*, haec ratio est, *quia profecta a nobis gratia duplex solet reverti.*" In sts. 23, 24, and also at *T.M.* 402, Sp. seems also to have in mind the interpretations of the Graces found in E.K.'s gloss on April 109.[6]

As handmaids of Venus they appear also at 4.4.5, where Florimell is assigned to their care, at *Epith* 103, where they are associated with the Hours (cf. Van Winkle, p. 93), and at 2.8.6, where they are sisters of Cupid. With this last cf. *T.M.* 403, where they are "to light by Venus brought." Servius *loc. cit.*, Bocc. 3.22, and N.C. 4.13 mention the tradition that the Graces were daughters of Venus. Hence they could be considered as sisters of Cupid. Sp. is probably thinking of their association with Venus when he introduces them at 1.1.48, singing "Hymen io Hymen." The presence of the Graces at weddings was not unusual; cf. *Met.* 6.429; Claudian, *Epithalamium* 202–3. The Graces are also companions of the Muses (*S.C.* April 100,f.; June 25; *T.M.* 402); cf. *Theog.* 63–4. Sp. multiplies the number of the Graces and uses their name generally as an attribute of beauty. 2.3.25 and *Am.* 40 repeat the conceit which E.K. (on June 25) quotes from Sp.'s *Pageants*, "An hundred Graces on her eyelids sat." E.K. points out the source in Musaeus, *Hero and Leander* 63. "A thousand Graces masking in delight," and thousands more, are Cytherea's handmaids (*H.B.* 254).

HADES

Hades is usually mentioned as Pluto's realm, "griesly land," or "baleful bowre" (*S.C.* Oct. 29; 1.5.14; 4.3.12; 4.10.58). To it there is a "beaten broad highway" (2.7.21) and its gate gapes wide (2.7.24); cf. *Aen.* 6.127–9; *Met.* 4.439–40. Most of the elements of Sp.'s Hades are treated in separate articles. Here it remains to discuss the group of personified forces of evil and horror that confront the entrant at the gate of Hades (2.7.21,f.): Pain, Strife, Revenge, Despight, Treason, Hate, Jealousy, Fear, Sorrow, Shame, Care, Sleep, Death. The primary source is *Aen.* 6.273–81, the "cubilia Curae" at the entrance of Vergil's Hades. Here, among others, appear "Luctus," "Cura," "Metus," "Letum," "Discordia." Other passages of a similar sort, if different in spirit, have contributed. Statius, *Theb.* 7.40,f., places such figures as sentinals at the cave of Mars: "exsangues metus," "Insidiae," "geminumque tenens Discordia ferrum," "voltuque cruento Mors armata." Chaucer, *Kn. Tale* A 1995,f., has contributed "Contek, with bloody knife and sharp manace" (cf. st. 21.6–9) and perhaps "pale drede" and "colde dethe." Similar figures appear as the offspring of Erebus and Night in Cicero, *Nat. Deor.* 3.17, and N.C. 3.12; see *Night.* The Induction to *The Mirror for Magistrates* has probably also contributed, especially in suggesting the figure of Sorrow. In the Induction,

---

[6] E.K.'s citations here are misleading. His reference to "Theodontius" would lead one to Bocc., who cites him frequently. But Bocc. does not mention him in connection with the Graces and does not have E.K.'s explanation of why the Graces are three in number. This seems to come rather from Seneca, *De Beneficiis* 1.3: "Alii quidem videri volunt unam esse quae det beneficium, alteram quae accipiat, tertiam quae reddat." The latter part of E.K.'s note, in which he cites Bocc. directly, may owe something to *G.D.* 5.35, but is much closer to Servius, quoted above.

there are figures at the gate of Hell such as "Dread," "fell Revenge," "Misery," "greedy Care," and by him "heavy Sleep, the cousin of Death." Finally, the idea of introducing these figures before the gate of Mammon's cave, in an allegory of avarice, may well have come from Bocc , 8.6, who makes Vergil's House of Dis (*Aen*. 6.541) a house of riches, associates it with Dante's House of Dis (*Inferno* 8), and describes just such abstractions as Sp.'s as guarding it: "*Divitiis* ferrea civitas et custos Thesiphon (*sic*) ideo datur, ut ferreas *avarorum* mentes et truculentias eorundem circa custodiam et tenacitatem earum cognoscamus . . . In hac civitate scribit Dantes noster obstinatis inferri supplicia, quibus nulla proximi charitas, nullusque fuit amor in deum. Per aulam autem atque circumstantes multiplicium *curarum anxietatis* et augendae rei labores execrabiles atque perdendi formidines quibus anguntur in *divitias* hi ulco tendentes guttere, intelligendi sunt." Cf. *Pluto*.

HAMADRYADS 1.6.18.

At *V.G.* 146 Sp. translates "Hamadryadas" (*Culex* 95) as "country nymphs." Perhaps he is thinking more particularly of the meaning of their name when, at 1.6.18, he calls them "woody nymphs." They are identified as wood-nymphs by N.C., 5.11; Bocc., 7.14; Servius, *ad Aen*. 1.500. Cf. *Nymphs*.

HARPIES 2.12.36.

In calling the Harpies "prophets of sad destiny," Sp. has in mind *Aen* 3.225–62, where the Harpies, led by Celaeno, make dire prophecies to Aeneas Cf. *Celaeno*.

HATE 2.7.22; 4.10.32–36.

On 2.7.22 see *Hades;* on 4.10.32–36 see *Concord*.

HEBE *R.T.* 384–5; *H.L* 283; *Epith*. 405.

Hebe appears in Sp. not as cup-bearer of the gods, but as the wife of Hercules after his apotheosis (cf. *Theog*. 950–55; *Od*. 11. 601–4) and as a deity presiding over fertility, one of those to whom Sp. addresses his prayer for children (*Epith*. 405). In all cases Sp. probably has in mind the identification of Hebe with "Iuventus" (Cicero, *Nat. Deor*. 1.40; N.C. 2.5) and Bocc.'s interpretation of her (9.2) as "viriditas perpetua," which is always "joined to the deeds of famous men" like Hercules, and is also the power which makes for "the renewal of all things, leaves, flowers, and all seeds."

HEBRUS *V. G.* 181; 1.11.30.

The idea of including Hebrus among the healing waters (1.11.30) may have come from *Ecl*. 10.65 and Servius' note thereon, in which he speaks of Hebrus as having healing powers. On *V.G.* 181 see *Orpheus*.

HECATE 1.1.43; 7.6.3.

At 7.6.3 Hecate appears as a Titaness who survived the fall of the older order and was granted "all rule and principality" by Jupiter. Sp. is probably following *Theog.* 411–52 (S). From the passage at 1.1.43, it appears that Hecate is conceived as having great power in the lower world and also some particular power over dreams. Cf. *Aen.* 6.247, where Aeneas invokes "Hecaten, caeloque Ereboque potentem." N.C., 3.15, describes her as the daughter of Night, by some identified with Proserpina, with whom she shares many characteristics and powers. Among other things, she is patroness of magic and the black arts of potions and poisons. Also, she is goddess of dreams, "phantasmata . . . quae solebant vocare Hecataea, *eaque in varias formas se convertebant*" (cf. 1.1.44, 47–49).

HECTOR *V.G.* 503–4, 515–23, 526–8; *R.R.* 14; 2.9.45.

All of Sp.'s direct references to Hector are in his early translations and in all cases follow their originals fairly closely. The reference at 2.9.45 to the death of "young Hector" Upton refers to *Met.* 13.415 and *Aen.* 2.448.

HELEN *S.C.* July 145–8; 2.7.55; 3.9.35; 3.10.12; 4.11.19; *CCCHA* 920.

The fullest passage on Helen as the type of beauty and as the cause of the Trojan War is at 3.9.35. Cf. *Il.* 3.146–60. At 4.11.19 Sp. calls her the "Tyndarid lass"; cf. *Aen.* 2.601. *CCCHA* 920 alludes to the story of Stesichorus and Helen; cf. *Phaedrus* 343; *The Boke of the Courtier*, ed. Everyman, p. 308. At two points there are connecting links between the classical Helen and Sp.'s Hellenore. At 3.10.12 Hellenore's behavior when she sees Malbecco's castle burning is, as Sp. says, like that of Helen at the sack of Troy, *Aen.* 6. 511,f. (Upton). Again, at 3.9.30 the signs that Paridell makes to Hellenore are those which Paris makes to Helen in *Heroides* 17.87–8 (Upton). In a more general way also, Sp.'s treatment of Hellenore seems to be based on his conception of Helen. *Heroides* 17 is one of the most subtly erotic of Ovid's writings. N.C., 6.23, voices the tradition regarding her when he speaks of Helen as "scelerata vitae" and interprets Paris' choice of her as a giving away to lust. On *S.C.* July 45–8; 2.7.55; 3.9.34; 4.11.19 see *Paris*.

HELIADES *V.G.* 198.

Sp. is following *Culex* 127–30 without significant addition, but may also have in mind Ovid's account of "the Sun's sad daughters" and their metamorphosis, *Met.* 2.340,f. At *T.M.* 7–12, where he speaks of the Muses as mourning for the fall of their brother, Phaethon, he is apparently identifying them with the Heliades, as daughters of Apollo (see *Muses*) and may have the *V.G.* passage in mind.

HELICON *S.C.* April 42, June 60, Nov. 30; *T.M.* 5, 271; *V.P.* 4, 5; *Ded. Son.* 5; *Am.* 1.

At *S.C.* April 42, *T.M.* 271, and *Am.* 1, Sp. treats Helicon as a spring rather than as a mountain. He is following a medieval rather than the classical tradition. Herford (ed. *S.C.*, p. 116) cites Chaucer, *H.F.* 521 and *Anelida* 15; cf. also *Troilus* 3.1809; Lydgate, *Temple of Glas* 706. The phrase "horsefoot," *T.M.* 271, associates Helicon with Hippocrene, Castalia, and the story of Pegasus; see *Pegasus*. E.K. (on April 42) says that Helicon is both a spring and a mountain. Sp. may mean it as the latter at *Ded. Son.* 5. Helicon may be intended in the references to the Muses' spring at June 60; Nov. 30; *V.P.* 4, 5. This is probable in the light of such phrases as "Heliconian imps" (*Ded. Son.* 3) and "Heliconian maids" (2.12.31).

HELLE 3.11.30; 5.Pr.5; 7.7.32.

There is no classical authority for a story of Jove loving Helle in the shape of a ram (3.11.30); but an explanation can be constructed. According to the classical story of Phrixus and Helle, which Sp. uses at 5.Pr.5, a ram with golden fleece carried these two in safety away from Ino; cf. *Fasti* 3.851–76; N.C. 6.9; Bocc. 13.68. Helle fell from the ram into the Hellespont, whence its name (cf. 7.7.32). This ram is identified with the constellation Aries by Ovid, *loc. cit.*, and Hyginus, *P.A.* 2.20, who also connects Aries with Jove. The latter identification is carried further by Bocc. in a passage (4.68) which probably influenced 7.7.32 (see *Zodiac*). Bocc. shows how the influence of Aries toward benignity and vernal fertility coincides with the characteristics of Jove and reflects the procreative power of the ram as leader of the flock. These associations of Jove and Helle with Aries may lie behind Sp.'s story. He may also have seen an analogy between this and the Europa story which comes next in the list of Jove's amours (3.11.30).

HERCULES

On Hercules' birth and parentage see *Alcmena*. Sp. applies to him all the epithets conventional among the Latin poets: Alcides, Amphitryonid, Tirynthian, Oetean. Sp. twice refers to his twelve labors as a whole (1.11.27; 3.7.61) but devotes more particular attention to only six of them; see *Cerberus, Diomedes, Geryon, Hesperides, Hydra, Nemean Lion.* At 4.1.23 Sp. alludes to Hercules' fight with the Centaurs, but seems to confuse it with the battle of the Centaurs at the wedding of Pirithous (cf. "bloodie feast," "drunken soules"). He is probably following Bocc.'s similar confusion (13.1): "Centauros insolentes, volentesque Hippodamiam nuptiarum die surripere Pirithoo Hercules acri bello superavit." Classical references to Hercules' fighting the Centaurs are scanty and cryptic; cf. *Met.* 9.191, 12.536–41.

At 2.5.31 Sp. treats as one the oak, sacred to Jove, and the poplar, sacred to Hercules. There may be a confused memory of Servius, *ad Ecl.* 7.61, who says that the poplar was sacred to Hercules because he made of it a crown for himself when he returned from the lower world. For the episode of Nessus' shirt (1.11.27), Ovid offers the closest parallel (*Met.* 9.153). Sp.'s mention of the "bloodie verse," seems to be his own addition.

The use of Hercules at 5.1.2, with Bacchus and Artegal, as one of the early defenders of justice and virtue serves to indicate Sp.'s deeper attitude toward him and his myth. The passage probably follows Horace, *Odes* 3.3 (Gough, p. 167), who mentions Hercules and Bacchus as upholders of justice. Sp. makes a good deal of Hercules' death on Mount Oeta, his apotheosis, and his union with Hebe in paradise (*R.T.* 381; 5.8.2; *H.L.* 283; cf. *T.M.* 461). The best classical authority on this is *Met.* 9.229–72, 400,f.; cf. also *Theog.* 950–5; *Od.* 11.601–4. On Hercules' final exaltation, Bocc. comments, "Ideo fictum est quantumque quia pereat corpus viri egregii, fama nomenque eius perpetuae iungitur iuventuti" (13.1). Cf. *Hebe.* On 2.10.11 see *Albion;* on 3.12.7; 4.10.27 see *Hylas;* on 5.5.24; 5.8.2 see *Iole.*

HERMES 7.6.19, 22, 32. See *Mercury.*

HESIONE ("IXIONE") *V.G.* 489–90.

Sp. apparently had before him Bembo's reading of *Culex* 300, "hunc rapuit serva" (Emerson, p. 112). A fuller version of the story of Hesione and Telamon is given at *Met.* 11.211,f., but one may doubt whether Sp. went to it. The form "Ixione" may be laid to Sp. himself or to the printer; cf. Renwick, *Compl.*, p. 270.

HESPERIDES 2.7.54; *Am.* 77.

Sp. refers to them simply as Atlas' daughters, for which he had authority in N.C. 7.7. In both passages the Hesperides and their apples, won by Hercules, are linked with Atalanta and her apples. The same association is made by N.C., *l.c.*, who may be taken as the source of both allusions. N.C. quotes *Aen.* 4.480–5, which mentions their garden, and Lucan 9.365–7, which speaks of Hercules' theft of the apples.

HESPERUS (VESPER) *V.G.* 315–16; 1.2.6; 1.7.30; 3.4.51; 7.6.9; *Epith.* 95, 286; *Proth.* 164.

In accord with classical usage, Hesperus, or Vesper, is both the morning and the evening star. At 1.2.6 he is the morning star, herald of "dawning light"; cf. *Fasti* 5.419–20. He is the evening star at *V.G.* 315–16, which translates *Culex* 203, and at 3.4.51. At *Epith.* 286,f. Hesperus, as the evening star, is associated with Venus, "the lampe of love"; cf. Van Winkle, p. 113. On *Proth.* 164 Jortin cites Seneca, *Hippol.* 749; *Aen.* 8.589; *Il.* 5.5. At 7.6.9 Vesper becomes Cynthia's page.

HIPPOLYTUS 1.5.37–39; 5.8.43.

Sp.'s telling of the Hippolytus myth does not agree with any one classical version, as S.'s discussion shows. He seems to be following Bocc.'s chapter on Hippolytus (10.50), which may be summarized as follows. Hippolytus gave his whole life to hunting and "with a constant heart spurned all women. He was loved by his stepmother, Phaedra, who, when she found that he would not requite her desire, accused him before Theseus." Theseus, "overcome by rage, prayed for his son's death." As a result, Hippolytus, fleeing in his chariot, encountered some sea-monsters ("phocae"), who so frightened his horses that they escaped control, overturned the car, and dragged Hippolytus, who was tangled in the reins, over cliffs and rough places, so that "pro mortuo a circumvicinis collectus sit." He was restored to life by Aesculapius. Bocc. here supplies all the material of Sp.'s version, in Sp.'s order, except two details: that Phaedra killed herself with a knife, and that Theseus, with Diana's help, gathered up Hippolytus' remains. Both of these points seem to be peculiar to Sp., but for the latter he may have received a suggestion from *Aen.* 7.765–69. At 5.8.43 Sp. singles out for use in a simile one striking feature of the story, Hippolytus' flight and death; Riedner, p. 111, cites *Met.* 15.497–9, 524.9.

HIPPOMENES 2.7.54.

The youth who captured Atalanta with the golden apples. S. explains the phrase, "Euboean young man," by showing, from Apollodorus and Hesiod, that Hippomenes was the son of Amphidamas, a king of Chalcis, on the island of Euboea. No more direct explanation appears.

HIPPONOE, HIPPOTHOE 4.11.50,51. See *Nereids*.

HORROR 2.7.23. See *Hades*.

HOURS 7.7.45; *Epith*. 98–102.

The idea of introducing the Hours in the pageant of the Seasons (7.7.45) probably comes from *Met.* 2.23–30, which describes the Hours, Day, Month, Year, and Seasons about the throne of Phoebus. Sp.'s versions of the parentage of the Hours (Jove and Night, 7.7.45; Day and Night, *Epith*. 98) are his own, but he is manifestly working from their connection with divisions of time. He may have got a suggestion from Bocc., 4.4, who makes them daughters of Sol and Cronis (Time) and says that this is because "they are made from a definite measurement of time by the progress of the sun." Sp.'s train of thought was similar. The role of the Hours as "porters of Heaven's gate" (7.7.45) is supported by *Il.* 5.749 (S) and *Fasti* 1.125. At *Epith*. 100–2 the Hours are said to control the seasons and to have the power of making and preserving all that is fair in the world. This latter idea is not suggested by classical sources, but is found in N.C., 4.16, who says that they stand for "rerum omnium abundantia," and that their names indicate their power to make things grow, and also that "Horae fructus ipsi sunt, quas semper fere poetae una cum Venere at cum Gratiae semper certe coniunxerunt" (cf. *Epith*. 103–4).

HYACINTHUS 3.6.45; 3.11.37.

The story of Apollo's love for Hyacinthus, which lies behind both of these allusions, is told at *Met.* 10.162–219. Cf. also *Met.* 13.394–8, where the purple flower, which Sp. calls a pansy, is described.

HYADES 3.1.57.

Sp. is following classical tradition in speaking of the Hyades as "moist"; cf. *Aen.* 1.744, 3.516. N.C. 4.7 is the authority for calling them the daughters of Atlas. The reference to their "weary drove" may derive from *Fasti* 5.165, "Pars Hyadum toto de grege nulla latet."

HYDRA *R.R.* 10; *V.B.* 10; 1.7.17; 2.12.23; 6.12.32.

At 1.7.17 Sp. follows classical tradition in describing the Hydra as "long fostered in Lerna lake," and as having "many heads out budding ever new." Cf. *Aen.* 8.300 (S); *Met.* 9.69–74. But no classical source mentions Stremona in this connection. Upton considers this an alternate form for Strymon, supposed to designate Thrace. At 6.12.32 the Blatant Beast reminds Sp. of the Hydra, hell-born, with a thousand heads. Sp. goes beyond the most extravagant classical statements on the number of the Hydra's heads. The association of the Hydra with hell, easy for Sp., may come from *Aen.* 6.576–7. *R.R.* 10 and *V.B.* 10 translate *Ant. Rome* 10.6 and *Songe* 10.11–12, respectively. On the "spring-headed hydras" (2.12.23), Winst. (*F.Q. II*, p. 289) cites Olaus Magnus 21.44. Bocc. 13.1 also mentions the tradition that the Hydra was a sea-monster.

HYLAS 3.12.7; 4.10.27.

Hercules and Hylas are among the famous friends in the Garden of Venus (4.10·27). 3.12.7 alludes to Hercules' search for the lost boy in a manner which recalls Theocritus 13.58–60 and *Ecl.* 6.43–4.

HYMEN *V.G.* 395; 1.1.48; *Epith.* 24–6, 140, 255, 405.

Except for *Epith.* 24–6, where Sp. speaks of Hymen's mask, his use of the god of marriage is entirely classical. The allusion at *V.G.* 395 is determined by *Culex* 247. The pagan cry, "Io Hymen," occurs at 1.1.48 and *Epith.* 140; cf. Catullus 61, where it is used in the refrain. On the use of Hymen in *Epith.* see Van Winkle's full notes, pp. 80–81, 96–7.

HYPERION *V.G.* 156; *Mui.* 51.

At *V.G.* 156, which translates *Culex* 101, Hyperion's name is used to denote the sun. The phrase "Hyperions fierie childe" (*Mui.* 51) follows the manner of *Met.* 4.192, 241, where "Hyperione natus" is a periphrasis for Apollo.

HYPSIPYLE 2.10.56. See *Argonautica*.

IDA *V.G.* 505; *S.C.* July 57–64, 146, Aug. 138; 2.7.55; 2.8.6; 2.12.52; 3.9.36; 3.11.34; 7.7.41.

Ida is mentioned as a mountain "where the gods love to repair" (2.12.52). Sp. probably did not distinguish between the two Idas. 2.8.6, which represents Cupid as at home on Ida with Venus and the Graces, may have been arrived at from the association of Venus with Ida (*Homeric Hymn to Aphrodite* 68; *Aen.* 12.411–12). On *S.C.* July 57–64 see Herford's quotation of a source in Mantuan (ed. *S.C.*, p. 144). *V.G.* 505 translates *Culex* 311–12. On *S.C.* July 146, Aug. 238; 2.7.55; 3.9.36 see *Paris;* on 3.11.24 see *Ganymede;* on 7.7.41 see "Capricornus" under *Zodiac.*

IGNORANCE *T.M.* 188–92, 259,f., 311,f.

With the lists of the offspring of Night in Hesiod, *Theog.* 211,f.; Cicero, *Nat. Deor.* 3.17; Claudian, *In.Rufinum* 1.28,f., and N.C. 3.12 (cf. *Night*) as precedents, Sp. adds to Night's progeny two figures of his own, Sloth and Ignorance. He is following at least the spirit of N.C.'s interpretation of Night (*loc. cit.*): "From Night are said to be born all the plagues mentioned above, since the *Ignorance* of mortals, which is *the Night of the mind*, is the parent and nurse of nearly all the calamities that afflict human beings. . . . All these things derive from ignorance." As the offspring of Night, Ignorance appropriately has his home in "the blacke abyss" (260, cf. 189) and was fed on Furies' milk (261). Continuing in the same manner, he creates additional personified abstractions as the offspring of Ignorance, "by him begotten of fowle Infamy": Error, Folly, Spight (*T.M.* 311–18).

INACHUS *T.M.* 447; 2.9.56; 4.11.15.

In all three passages Inachus is remembered primarily as one celebrated and famous. With the phrase "renowned above the rest" (4.11.15) cf. N.C.'s "celeberrimum praeterea" (8.22) and cf. Horace, *Odes* 2.3.21–4, where, as in Sp., the name is used as a sign of high birth and ancient fame.

INFAMY *T.M.* 316. See *Ignorance.*

INO 4.11.13; 5.Pr.5; 5.8.47.

The classical source for the story of Ino's madness, and of her son, Palaemon, is *Met.* 4.416–542 (S). Sp. may be using it, but is probably also following N.C., 8.4, who quotes those parts of Ovid's story that Sp. uses. N.C. adds what is not in Ovid, that Palaemon presides over sailors (cf. 4.11.13.6). The allusion at 5.8.47 can hardly be explained by reference to Ovid alone; but N.C. gives several confusing versions of the story from which Sp. might have gathered that Ino "threw her husbands murdred infant out." On 5.Pr.5 see *Helle.*

IOLE 5.5.24; 5.8.2.

In the first passage Sp. points out, in a simile, the connection between the story of Hercules' voluntary degradation and his own story of Artegal and Radigund. Mustard (*MLN*, 20.127) traced the use of Iole for Omphale to Tasso, *G.L.* 16.3. But Bocc., 13.1, makes the same confusion and his version of the story is the closest parallel to Sp.: 'Eurito occiso, Iolem obtinuit [Hercules]. Huius enim amore ardens ea iubente leonis spolium et clavam deposuit, sertis et unguentis et purpura annulisque usus est, et quod turpius, inter pedissequas amatae iuvenis sedens, penso suscepto venit."

IPHIMEDIA 3.11.42.

The source is *Met.* 6.116–17, but Ovid's allusion is rather cryptic. Regius' note (Burmann 2.390), which Sp. may have seen, explains: "Neptune came in the form of a flowing river, Enipeus, to Iphimedia, wife of Alous."

IRIS *Mui.* 93; 3.11.47; 5.3.25.

Sp. twice compares the vari-colored bow of Iris (cf. *Aen.* 4.701) to wings, of Cupid and of Clarion (3.11.47; *Mui.* 93). 5.3.25 is a description of the rainbow of the "daughter of Thaumantes." The form "Thaumantes" may have been caught from the Latin, "Thaumantias" (*Aen.* 9.5; *Met.* 4.480), or from Bocc. 9.1, "Iris, quam Thaumantis fuisse filiam voluere, id est, admirationis, eo quod sit coloribus et apparitione mirabilis" (cf. 5.3.25.4).

IRUS *T.M.* 447.

He is used as a type of the lowly in birth and breeding, contrasted with Inachus. Irus was the beggar who got his name "because he ran on errands whenever anyone might bid him" (*Od.* 18.1,f.). Cf. the similar use of Irus in the Induction to *The Mirror for Magistrates*, 294.

ISIS 5.7.2,f.

Sp.'s use of Isis and Osiris is based on Plutarch, *De Iside*, and Diodorus 1.11,f. (cf. Riedner, pp. 61–62; Gough, pp. 247–50), with perhaps some additional suggestions from N.C. 5.13. He uses his sources with freedom and independence. The conception of Osiris as a just king (st. 2) who, because of his reputation, afterwards became a god of justice, is found in Plutarch 13, Diodorus 1.17, and N.C. Isis as "that part of justice which is equity" is probably founded on Plutarch 3 and Diodorus 1.14, where she is said to have "caused men to practice justice among themselves." The identification of Osiris with the sun and of Isis with the moon is in Diodorus 1.11 and Plutarch 52. For the description of the character and habits of Isis' priests, Sp. is indebted mainly to Plutarch, 2–6, who tells of their austere and continent rule, their linen robes, their abstinence from flesh and wine. Sp. contradicts Plutarch in giving them long hair; he may be remembering N.C.'s remark (noted by Lemmi, p. 274) that, in commemoration of his triumphs, Osiris commanded that men's hair should be worn long. Sp. may also owe something to N.C.'s description of the *galli* (9.5), the priests of Rhea, with whom Isis was identified. The *galli* were vowed to chastity and were clothed in the habit of women. The crocodile (st. 7) may represent a memory of what Plutarch has to say about Typhon, the enemy of Isis and Osiris, and a symbol of the powers of disorder and confusion.

Plutarch says (ch. 50) that Typhon once assumed the form of a crocodile. Plutarch may also have given a suggestion for Britomart's dream (st. 12,f.). In ch. 81 he says that sleeping in the temple, near burning incense, is a stimulus to the "imaginative and prophetic part of dreams."

ISSE 3.11.38–39.1–5

Cupid drove Apollo to love a shepherd's daughter, Isse; and for her sake he tended her cattle, and for her sake he became "a cowherd vile . . . the servant of Admetus." This seems to be the meaning of these rather puzzling lines. For one explanation see Upton (Todd 5.93), who assumes that Isse is meant to be Admetus' daughter and cites Chaucer, *Troilus* 1.659–65 and *Amadis de Gaule* 1.36, which tell of Apollo's love for Admetus' daughter. But Sp. says that Isse was "a shepherds daughter." If he meant that the shepherd was Admetus, he may have been influenced in his strange jumble by a passage in N.C. (4.10) which presents Admetus as a shepherd. Sp. probably took his start from *Met.* 6.124, but he was either puzzled or napping at the time.

ITIS *V.G.* 402–4. See *Philomela.*

IULUS 3.9.43.

Most of Sp.'s material here could have been gathered from scattered passages in *Aen.* (1.288, 6.364, 6.789). But there is no reference in Vergil to quarrels as the cause of Iulus' migration to Alba Longa. This could have been gathered from Bocc.'s account (6.54) of Iulus' wars and the founding of Alba Longa. Bocc. (6.55–73) gives a complete genealogy from Iulus to Romulus, which may have helped Sp.

IXION 1.5.35; 7.6.29.

Ixion appears in Sp., as conventionally in the classics, as one of those punished in Hades; cf. *Aen.* 6.601; *Met.* 4.461. At 1.5.35.1–6 Sp. has the same order of names as N.C. (6.16), an order which is not paralleled in the classics. On Ixion N.C. (*loc. cit.*) quotes lines from Tibullus (1.3.73–4) which are rather close to 1.5.35.1–2: "Illic Iunonem tentare Ixionis ausi Versantur celeri noxia membra rota."

JANUS 4.10.12; *Am.* 4.

Sp. thinks of Janus as a door-keeper (4.10.12) and of his gate as the entrance to the new year (*Am.* 4). In the former passage he plays on the idea of Janus' double face in the creation of his own character, Doubt, the warder of the Temple of Venus. Cf. *Fasti* 1.63,f. Cf. also E.K.'s remarks on Janus in the "Generall Argument."

JARRE 2.4.41.

Sp.'s "Jarre" is closely associated with his own Ate and with the classical peronifications of Discord, Eris, Litigium, Discordia. In using Jarre in the genealogy of

Pyrochles and Cymochles, he may have been influenced by *Theog.* 223,f., where Eris, descended from Nemesis and Night, is the parent of Toil, Grief, Wars, Lawlessness, and others. Bocc.'s Litigium (1.3) may also have given suggestions (Upton). She was born from the womb of Chaos while Daemogorgon was in the cave of Aeternitas (cf. 2.4.41.9).

JASON R.R. 10; 2.12.44. See *Argonautica.*

JEALOUSY 2.7.22; 3.11.1. See *Hades.*

JOVE

Mutability makes a point of the conflicting traditions as to Jove's birthplace (7.7.52). N.C. makes the same point at the beginning of his chapter on Jove (2.1): "Modo in Creta, modo Thebis, modo in Arcadia, modo apud Messenios natus esse dicitur." A part of the Cretan tradition is the story of Amalthea, his nurse "in tender years," and her goat (7.7.41); see "Capricornus" under *Zodiac.* In the description of Jove at *Mui.* 308–12, Sp. follows *Met.* 6.74, "Iovis est regalis imago," but elaborates to heighten the impression of his majesty. There are reminiscences of the Homeric Zeus at *M.H.T.* 1228 and 7.6.22, in the mention of his "black eyebrow," and at 7.6.30, in the shaking of his "nectar-dewed locks," which made the world quake; cf. *Il.* 1.528–30 (Riedner, p. 30); *Met.* 1.179–80. In accord with classical tradition, Jove is "father of the gods" (*T.M.* 55; 7.6.15), king of the gods (7.6.14), "heavens king" (1.5.43). The eagle is his royal bird (*R.R.* 17; *V.W.V.* 4; 2.11.43); cf. *Ganymede.* He "doth true justice deale to his inferiour gods" (5.7.1). He is the god of political justice and the god of kings as well as king of the gods. This conception appears clearly at *M.H.T.* 1225, is behind E.K.'s gloss on April 50, and is in the treatment of Jove in *Mut.* Cf. *Il.* 2.196–206 (quoted by E.K.); *Aen.* 6.129–30; Horace, *Odes* 3.1.5–8; N.C., 2.1, who says, "Regibus illis qui ab ipso fuerunt instituti, et parendi sibi et subditis nationibus imperandi legis tradidit." Related is the idea of Jove as patron of Rome (*V.W.V.* 11); cf. *Fasti* 2.69 (S), 2.667–8) Servius, *ad Aen.* 9.446, on Jupiter Capitolinus. In his astrological character as a benign and kindly influence, he appears at 3.6.2 (cf. 2.12.51, "joviall"). Sp. could find this developed by Bocc., 2.2, and N.C., 2.1, p. 101.

Mention is made of Jove's palace as a place distinct from the heavens as a whole (*M.H.T.* 1227; 1.4.17; 4.11.28; 5.1.9; 7.6.15; 7.6.23), but one also finds the phrase "house of Jove" used as synonymous with the sky (1.5.19; 3.4.51; 5.7.8). This is part of the conception of Jove as god of the sky (6.10.22), as ruler of Night and Day (1.5.42; cf. 1.5.19; 1.7.23; 3.1.57), commonly identified with the sky in classical poetry; cf. *Il.* 15.189–92; Horace, *Odes* 1.1.26; *Geo.* 1.418. In this capacity he is called the Thunderer (1.4.11; 1.5.42; 2.6.10; 3.11.30); cf. *Fasti* 2.69, "Iuppiter Tonans." His thunderbolts appear habitually as a sign of his vengeance on mortal sins. The storm is an expression of his wrath (1.1.6); cf. Lucretius 1.251; *Geo.* 2.325 (Jortin). The stars are "th' eternall lampes, wherewith high Jove doth light the lower world" (3.1.57). He assigned to Cynthia sovereignty over "nights burning lamp," the moon (7.6.12).

The amorous side of Jove's nature is also prominent in Sp.'s conception of him. This is developed most fully in the catalogue of his amours at 3.11.30–35; see *Aegina, Alcmena, Antiopa, Astery 2, Danae, Europa, Helle, Leda, Mnemosyne, Proserpina, Semele.* Jove is father of Cupid by Venus (1.Pr.3; see *Cupid*); of Mars (*R.R.* 11); of Mercury (*M.H.T.* 1299; see *Maia*). Lucifera, in her pride, claimed him as her father (1.4.11); cf. the similar case of Alexander (1.5.48; see *Ammon*). At *R.T.* 369 Jove is called the father of Eternity. This bit of original myth may spring from the idea expressed by Bocc., 11.1, that Jove is the giver of fame and immortality for the brave deeds of heroes.

Finally, there is room in the midst of these varied conceptions for the idea that Jove was, anagogically considered, a symbol of the true Godhead. At 7.6.21 he addresses "ye sonnes of God," and at *H.H.B.* 181 the thunder and lightning usually associated with Jove are under the throne of God. Cf. Bocc. 2.2: "Volunt enim aliqui et graves viri quod idem Iuppiter sonet quod iuvans pater, quod soli vero Deo convenit. Ipse enim vere pater est et ab aeterno fuit et erit in sempiternum."

See also *Aesculapius, Castor, Cupid, Eurynome, Giants, Golden Chain, Hercules, Hours, Latona, Litae, Memory, Olympus, Prometheus, Titan.*

JUNO *Mui.* 95; 1.4.17; 1.5.35; 2.12.13; 3.11.33; 7.7.26; *Epith.* 390–7.

Juno occupies a rather unimportant place in Sp.'s mythology. All that he says of her is in accord with classical tradition. Thus she is "the queen of heaven" (1.5.35), whose special dominion is the air (7.7.26). This is supported by N.C. 2.4; Bocc. 9.1; Servius, *ad Aen.* 4.122. At *Epith.* 390–7 Sp. calls Juno the patroness of "the lawes of wedlock" and goddess of childbirth; cf. Van Winkle's citations, pp. 122–23, and Bocc., 9.1, who says, "parturientium dicta est . . . a parturientibus sub Lucinae et Iunonis nomine invocari, eius muneris esse dicebant . . . ad accelerandas partus salutare." She is mentioned with her peacock at *Mui.* 95 and in her chariot drawn by peacocks at 1.4.17. Here Sp. is probably following *Met.* 2.531–3 (S). The comparison of Lucifera with Juno carries with it the connotation of pride which, partly by reference to her sacred peacock, was made an element of Juno's character by Bocc., 9.1, and N.C., 2.4. On 1.5.35 see *Ixion;* on 2.12.13 see *Latona;* on 3.11.33 see *Semele.*

LACHESIS 4.2.48, 51. See *Fates.*

LAERTES *V.G.* 533.

Ulysses is named as "Laertes son," following *Culex* 327.

LAESTRYGONES *V.G.* 538.

"Blacke Laestrigones, a people stout." Sp. translates *Culex* 330, where his text probably read "atros," instead of "atrox" (see Plésent, p. 83; Emerson, p. 113).

LAOMEDIA 4.11.51. See *Nereids*.

LAOMEDON 2.11.19.

The idea of Laomedon's horses bred of Phoebus' race seems to represent a blend of the horses of the Sun (*Met.* 2.153–5) and the horses given by Zeus to Tros and by him to Laomedon (*Il.* 5.265,f.). Bocc., 6.6, says that Laomedon promised to Hercules his horses "born of divine seed." Sp. may have associated these with Phoebus, thinking of Laomedon's dealings with Phoebus at the building of Troy (cf. *Met.* 11.200,f.). There is a possibility that the blend arose from a misreading of Spondanus' translation of *Il.* 5.640–1: "Qui quondam huc veniens gratia *equorum Laomedontis Sex solis* cum navibus et viris paucioribus."

LAPITHS *V.G.* 41–2; 4.1.23; 6.10.13.

V.G. 41–2 is based on *Culex* 29. For the other references, S. cites *Met.* 12.210, but this tells more of Theseus fighting the Centaurs; the Lapiths figure but little, whereas in Sp. they are most prominent. Sp. remembered the episode chiefly as a victory of the Lapiths over the Centaurs who, for him, would represent powers of evil. For this emphasis he is probably indebted to N.C. 7.4, where he could also find his details.

LATINUS 3.9.42, 43. See *Aeneas*.

LATONA *S.C.* April 86; *V.G.* 13, 377–80; 2.12.13; 4.7.30; 6.2.25.

The story of Latona's flight from Juno, her taking refuge on Delos, and her giving birth to Apollo and Diana, appears most fully at 2.12.13. S. cites *Homeric Hymn to Delian Apollo*. N.C.'s version (9.6) is closest to Sp.: "No place would give a refuge to Latona except the island of Delos. It at that time was unstable and at times hid under the waves; but when the time of childbirth came to Latona, Neptune ordered it to stand firm and give a place for the birth." At *V.G.* 13 and 6.2.25 Apollo is referred to as Latona's son, and at 4.7.30 Diana is called Latona's daughter, and both together are "Latonaes seede" at *S.C.* April 86. On *V.G.* 377–80 see *Tityus*.

LEANDER *H.L.* 231.

The suggestion for a group of examples of the power of Love at this point comes from *Symposium* 178–80; but Leander is not mentioned there. Sp. substitutes him for Alcestis. S. cites Musaeus, *Hero and Leander;* cf. also *Heroides* 18, 19.

LEDA *R.T.* 386; 3.11.32; 7.7.34; *Proth.* 42–4.

3.11.32, describing Jove's seduction of Leda, in the shape of a swan, is elaborated from *Met.* 6.109. The same episode, with some of the same imagery, is used at *Proth.* 42–4. *R.T.* 386 and 7.7.34 refer to Castor and Pollux as the "twins of Leda"; see *Castor*.

LEMNOS 4.5.4. See *Vulcan*.

LEO *S.C.* July 21, Dec. 57; *M.H.T.* 6; 5.Pr.6; 7.7.36; *Daph.* 165. See *Zodiac*.

LERNA LAKE 1.7.17; 5.11.32. See *Hydra*.

LETHE *S.C.* March 23; *V.G.* 337–42; *R.T.* 428–9; 1.3.36.

Except at *S.C.* March 23 (on which E.K.'s gloss offers sufficient explanation), Sp. has confused Lethe with Styx. 1.3.36, referring to Sansfoy's spirit as passing over Lethe into Hades, may well derive from *V.G.* 337–42, where, following *Culex* 214–17, Sp. represents the souls as coming to Lethe and being ferried over by Charon. The same confusion, which occurs also in the classics (cf. *Theb.* 4.622–4), may serve to explain *R.T.* 428–9, where it is said that Thetis dipped Achilles "in Lethe lake."

LIAGORE 3.4.41; 4.11.51.

She is named among the Nereids at 4.11.51 and at 3.4.41 she is the beloved of Apollo, to whom he taught leechcraft, and by him the mother of Paeon. Upton explains this passage as influenced by the story of Apollo and Oenone; cf. *Heroides* 5.139,f. (S). Sp. associated the powers of nourishing and healing with Nymphs in general; cf. 4.11.52.9 and *Nymphs*.

LIBRA 5.1.11; 7.7.38. See *Zodiac*.

LIMBO LAKE 1.2.32; 3.10.54.

Limbo is not originally classical, but Sp. makes it a part of the classical Hades. The idea of Limbo as classical begins, according to the *N.E.D.*, in T. Howell's *Devises* (1581). Closer to Sp. is Stanyhurst's translation of *Aen.*, where he translates "Orco" (2.398) as "Limbo." The phrase "Limbo lake" occurs before Sp. only in Phaer's translation. He translates *Aen.* 3.386, "For Circe's isle must first be seen and lands of Limbo lake" (*The XIII Bookes of Aeneidos* ... Translated into English Verse by Thomas Phaer, London 1584, Bk. III, G. iv, *verso*). Sp.'s use of Limbo is thus a direct result of his use of Elizabethan translations of Vergil which used the Christian term as an equivalent for Latin *Orcus* and *infernus*.

LINUS *R.T.* 333.

He is represented with Orpheus in the Elysian fields; cf. *Ecl.* 4.55–6, 6.67. As Vergil, in the latter passage, is thinking of his dead friend, the poet Gallus, so Sp. is thinking of Sidney.

LISIANISSA 4.11.50. See *Nereids*.

LITAE 5.9.31–32.

Sp.'s Litae have the same parents, Jove and Themis, and the same names as Hesiod gives to the Hours (*Theog.* 901–3). For this confusion of Litae and Hours,

N.C. is partly responsible. At 2.1 N.C. mentions the Litae in close connection with Themis and discusses their activities in regard to the prayers of kings in terms which parallel st. 32.1–4. At 4.16 he attaches similar meaning to the Hours, quotes *Theog. loc. cit.*, and shows that their names mean justice, law, and peace, which well suits Sp.'s purpose in his passage on the Litae.

LUCINA 2.1.53; 3.6.27; *Epith.* 383, 394.

Sp. uses Lucina in the classical way, as the goddess of childbirth, and at *Epith.* 383 and 394 connects her with Diana and with Juno. Lucina presided at the birth of Ruddymane (2.1.53), but was not needed when Chrysogone bore Amoret and Belphoebe (3.6.27). Cf. *Fasti* 2.449,f., 3.255 (S). Her nature and powers are explained by N.C., 4.1. See *Diana, Juno.*

LYAEUS 3.1.51.

A name for Bacchus, here standing for wine. See *Bacchus.*

MAENADS *V G.* 171–6; 5.8.47. See *Agave* 2.

MAIA *S.C.* March 17; *M.H.T.* 1257; 4.3.42; 7.6.16; *Epith.* 307–10.

For *Epith.* 307–10 the chief source is probably *Homeric Hymn to Hermes* (cf. Van Winkle, p. 115). There she is "a shy goddess" (cf. *Epith.* 306); she dwells in a shadowy cave and Jove comes to her in the night (cf. *Epith.* 300). For the use of the Acidalian brook here, Sp. may possibly have received a suggestion from N.C. 5.5, where he says that Maia bore Mercury in Arcadia at a place where there were three fountains. E.K.'s gloss on March 17 is, in spite of his citing Macrobius, probably based on Bocc. 4.35, "Ei quidem, ut ait Macrobius, mense Maio eo quod ab ea denominatum putarent." On *M.H.T.* 1257; 4.3.42; 7.6.16 see *Mercury.*

MARS

Sp.'s Mars appears in four aspects, as the bloody god of war, as the adulterous lover of Venus, as the "gentle knight" and courtly lover of Venus, as the planet.

As god of war, Sp.'s Mars is quite conventional, and, as with classical Latin writers, his name is sometimes used as a generic term for war (*S.C.* Oct. 39; 2.1.8). Poetry and the Muses are powers that arouse the Martial spirit (1.116.–7); cf. *Aen.* 6.165 and Sp.'s remarks on the Irish bards (*View*, Todd 8.394–7). Mars is the founder of the Roman race (*R.R.* 11). Here Sp. changes *Ant. Rome* 11 and follows either Ovid (*Fasti* 1.40, 3.24) or Bocc. (9.41), who names Mars as father of Romulus and emphasizes his warlike character in connection with the Romans, his descendents.

The conception of Mars as the adulterous lover of Venus (*Mui.* 369–73; 2.6.35; 3.6.24; 3.11.36; 3.11.44; 4.5.5) is based on the story of Mars and Venus and the snares of Vulcan, which appears in most detail at *Mui.* 369–73. The ultimate source of the story is *Od.* 8. 266–369 (S), but Sp. is a good deal closer to *Met.* 4.176–89.

In the hands of medieval doctors and poets of courtly love, the Mars of the above myth became Mars "of knighthoode welle," the type of the courtly lover in the service and worship of the symbol of beauty, Venus. Cf. Chaucer, *Complaint of Mars* and *Complaint of Venus* (especially *Mars* 43–4, 75, 187, 275; *Venus* 9–12). The influence of these two poems alone may account for Sp.'s including Mars in the general invocation at 1.Pr.2–4, not as the fierce god of war, nor as the adulterer, but as "Mart, in loves and gentle jollities arraid." Mars thus becomes a patron of the lover-knights of Sp.'s romance.

Mars appears as the planet, without particular characterization, at 5.Pr.8; 7.7.52; *Am.* 60.

MEDEA *V.G.* 397–400; 2.12.44–45; 5.8.47. See *Argonautica*.

MEDUSA *R.T.* 647; 3.9.22; 3.11.42; 4.11.13; *Epith.* 190.

3.11.42 tells of the conception of Pegasus by Medusa and Neptune in the form of a winged horse. *Met.* 6.119, Sp.'s original source, says Neptune took the form of a winged bird, but a note on the line by Regius (Burmann 2.391) says, "Neptune, changed into a horse, lay with Ceres and Medusa." The story of the birth of Pegasus from Medusa's blood (*R.T.* 647) begins in *Theog.* 280–6 and is found at *Met.* 4.785–6, Fulgentius, *Myth.* 1.21, Bocc. 10.27, and N.C. 7.11. The conquest of Medusa by Perseus was probably in Sp.'s mind when he spoke of the "fatall brood" of Phorcys (Medusa's father) "by whom those old heroes wonne such fame" (4.11.13). He would have found the complete genealogy of Phorcys, with mention of the heroes, at *Theog.* 270–336. On 3.9.22 see *Aegide*.

MEGAERA *T.M.* 164. See *Furies*.

MELANTHO 3.11.42.

Sp. refers to her as "Deucalions daughter." He is expanding *Met.* 6.120. Regius' note on the line (Burmann 2.391–2) explains what Sp. could not have gathered from Ovid alone: "Melantho was Deucalion's daughter, to whom Neptune came in the shape of a dolphin."

MELITE 4.11.49. See *Nereids*.

MELPOMENE *S.C.* Oct. 112, Nov. 53; *Mui.* 10, 413; *T.M.* 115–174. See *Muses*.

MEMORY *R.T.* 368; 1.11.5; 3.3.4; 4.11.10. See *Muses*.

MENIPPE 4.11.51. See *Nereids*.

MERCURY *R.T.* 666; *M.H.T.* 1246,f.; 2.12.41; 4.3.42; 7.6.14, 16,f.; 7.7.51.

With considerable elaboration, Mercury appears in his classical role as messenger of the gods at *M.H.T.* 1246,f. The passage as a whole has resemblances to *Theb.* 1.292–311; *Aen.* 1.297–307, 4.238–46; *Met.* 1.668–77. At *M.H.T.* 1258 and 7.6.17

Mercury is represented as winged. With the phrase "wingd-foot" (7.6.17) cf. "ali-pedus," *Met.* 4.756, 11.312. He takes on a new shape (*M.H.T.* 1266); this was his practice in several of the myths associated with him; cf. *Met.* 1.676, 2.686,f. Mercury's hat (*M.H.T.* 1279–91) is mentioned by the Latin poets cited above, but they do not say, as Sp. does at length, that it has the power of making him invisible. Sp. is apparently confusing or identifying this hat with Pluto's hat of darkness, which Mercury lent to Perseus (N.C. 7.11; Apollodorus 2.4.3; cf. Renwick,*Compl.*, p. 244). Sp. links with the powers of his hat the "cunning theeveries" (*M.H.T.* 1287) traditionally associated with Mercury. On his wand, mentioned at *M.H.T.* 1291,f.; 2.12.41; 4.3.42; 7.6.18, see *Caduceus*. It is chiefly through the powers of Caduceus that Mercury figures as a peacemaker (*R.T.* 666; cf. 4.3.42). Cf. N.C. 5.5, "Quidem iniunxerunt illi etiam bellicas caducateorum legationes, cum foederum et indutiarum illum inventorem fuisse inquiant." Cf. *Fasti* 5.665–6, "Pacis et ar-morum superis imisque deorum Arbiter." It is as messenger of the gods and as arbiter of peace that Mercury figures in 7.6.14,f. Here the conception of Mercury as a planet (cf. 7.7.44, 51) and as the god of classic myth are fused. On Mercury's birth and parentage see *Maia*. He is called "Maia's son" at *M.H.T.* 1257; 4.3.42; 7.6.16.

MERMAIDS *V.B.* 12; 2.12.17, 30–34.

There was no distinction in Sp.'s mind between mermaids and sirens. At *V.B.* 12 he translates "sirene" (*Songe* 12) as "mermaid," and at 2.12.30, f. mermaids have the rôle and character of the classical sirens. Bocc. (7.20), discussing the sirens, says that their lower part is like a fish, thus associating them with mermaids (cf. 2.12.30), whereas the classical sirens were part bird. With this conception of their nature, Sp. has altered the story of the metamorphosis of the sirens after their contest with the Muses (2.12.30); cf. Todd 4.196. The same identification of mermaids and sirens is found in Chaucer, *Romaunt of the Rose* 679–84. Sp.'s description of their dwelling, 2.12.30, probably follows *Aen.* 1.159–67 (Riedner, p. 72).

Sp. follows well established classical precedent when he introduces the mermaids, or sirens, as a part of the difficulties of Guyon's voyage. He probably had in mind *Od.* 12.37–54, 165–200; Ap. Rh. 4.891,f., and *Aen.* 5.864–5. In Sp.'s hands this material carries obvious and clearly marked ethical meaning. This was perhaps implicit in the classical versions; but the later commentators elaborated the allegory and made it of first importance. Bocc. (7.20) interprets the fish-like nature of the sirens as indicating "omnem libidinosam mulierum concupiscentiam." N.C., 7.13 (cf. Lemmi,p. 279),is more elaborate and closer to Sp. He associates their song with the sound of the sea (cf. st. 33) and says that "in order to capture the ambitious and those desirous of glory, in order to seduce the lustful, they sing of love. . . . I believe the Sirens' song and the Sirens themselves to be nothing other than voluptuous desire." They lead men to destruction because they represent that part of the soul which is irrational, and the powers of seduction that act on that part. "Incredible and almost divine prudence is needed if one will listen to the Sirens and yet be able to pass by unharmed."

MINERVA *Mui.* 261–352; 3.9.22

Minerva's place in Sp.'s pantheon is rather unimportant. She figures most prominently at *Mui.* 261–352, which, following *Met.* 6.1,f., tells of her contest with Arachne. *Mui.* 265–76, sketching the introduction for the story, summarizes *Met.* 6.5–69. At *Mui.* 305,f. Sp. begins to follow Ovid closely (*Met.* 6.70–82). Thence he takes his material for the "storie of the olde debate," Neptune and Minerva before the "twelve gods," the description of Neptune and his "challenge," the description of Minerva and her gift of the olive tree. At *Mui.* 327 Sp. leaves Ovid, elaborates the picture of the olive tree, and adds as his own the butterfly, thereby changing the end of the story; see *Arachne.* On *Mui.* 321 see *Aegide.* At 3.9.22 Minerva appears as the victor over Enceladus in the battle with the Giants; see *Enceladus.* Sp. does not refer to Minerva as the goddess of wisdom. Her warlike character is uppermost in both passages. The description at *Mui.* 321–3 resembles those at *V.B.* 15 and 4.1.14 of Bellona, with whom Sp. may at times have confused her; see *Bellona.*

MINOS *V.G.* 623–4, 627.

At *V.G.* 623–4 Sp. translates *Culex* 374–5, adding "to live in blisse forever." The "cruell judge" at 627 is probably Minos; cf. *Culex* 377.

MINOTAURS *M.H.T.* 1123; 3.10.40.

In both passages "Minotaures" are grouped with dragons, griffons, crocodiles, and others as "monstrous beasts." No direct source for such usage can be shown; but the same way of regarding the monsters of classic myth as one with monsters in general is found in Aelian and in Konrad Gesner's *Thierbuch.*

MNEMOSYNE 3.11.35.

One of the loves of Jove. Sp. is using *Met.* 6.114. In his references to Aegina, Mnemosyne, and the "Thracian maid" (Proserpina), he is even following Ovid's order.

MORPHEUS *V.B.* 15; 1.1.36; 1.1.39–44; 1.4.44; 2.7.25; 6.8.34.

The passage on the cave of Morpheus, 1.1.39–44, is a compound of several sources, chiefly *Met.* 11.590–650; *Theb.* 10.84–117; Chaucer, *B.D.* 135–194.[7] The cave is deep in the earth, far from day (st. 39); cf. *B.D.* 155; *Met.* 11.592–6; *Theb.* 10.85–8. It is washed by the Ocean (st. 39); this is not in the above sources and seems to have been suggested by N.C.'s statement (3.14) that Somnus is said to live in the ocean because sleep is caused by the rising of humours into the brain. The house has a double gate, one of ivory, one of silver (st. 40); cf. *Aen.* 6.893–8. A stream trickles down from a rock, making a lulling sound (st. 41); cf. *B.D.* 163; *Met.* 11.603–4. The messenger

[7] A. S. Cook, "The House of Sleep," *MLN*, 5.10–21, collected parallel passages from Ariosto, Politian, Chaucer, Statius, Ovid, Homer, and Vergil, but made no appraisal of their significance in relation to 1.1.39–44.

awakens Morpheus by threatening him with the "dreaded name of Hecate"; in Chaucer, Ovid, and Statius the name of Juno is used; see *Hecate*. In connection with the "diverse dreame" (st. 44), Sp. may have had in mind Bocc.'s discussion of dreams in a passage on Somnus (1.31). In speaking of the "insomnium," a false dream, like Sp.'s (in Chaucer, Ovid, and Statius the dream is true), he cites *Aen.* 6.896, which is in Sp.'s mind. At 2.7.25 there is further reference to the cave of Sleep, which indicates that for Sp. Morpheus and Sleep were interchangeable. In making them so, he was probably influenced by Chaucer, *loc. cit.*; in the classical sources Morpheus is a servant of Somnus. Sp. mentions two ways in which Sleep exerts his power, both classical. At 1.1.36 the "messenger of Morpheus on them cast sweet slombring deaw"; cf. *Theb.* 2.144, 5.199, 6.27; 10.111, where Sleep carries a horn from which he pours the dew of sleep. At 1.4.11 Morpheus' "leaden mace" is Sp.'s adaptation of the classical Somnus' sleep-bringing branch or wand; cf. *Aen.* 5.854; Silius Italicus 10.354–6.

MULCIBER 2.7.5; 3.11.26. See *Vulcan*.

MUSES

Sp. makes the Muses daughters of Apollo and Memory (*T.M.* 2, 57; 2.10.3; 3.3.4; *Epith.* 121; cf. E.K. on April 41). N.C. 4.10, p. 346 (Lemmi, p. 274) seems to be the authority for this: "Fuerunt . . . Musae in eius tutela creditae, quarum *dux et pater Apollo fuit existimatus.*" At *S.C.* June 66; *R.T.* 366; 4.11.10, he follows the classical tradition which makes Jove and Memory their parents; cf. *Theog.* 53,f.; Cicero, *Nat. Deor.* 3.21.

T.M. gives evidence for Sp.'s conception of the separate functions of the nine Muses. This seems to be based primarily on some mnemonic verses which, in Sp.'s time, were included among Vergil's works, and are quoted by N.C., 7.15. E.K. quotes twice from them, as Vergil's (on April 100, Nov. 52).

> Clio gesta canens transactis tempora reddit
> Melpomene tragico proclamat moesta boatu.
> Comica lasciva gaudet sermone Thalia.
> Dulciloquis calamos Euterpe flatibus urget.
> Terpischore affectus citharis movet: imperat: auget.
> Plectra gerens Erato saltat pede: carmine: vultu.
> Carmina Calliope libris heroica mendat.
> Urania poli motus scrutatur et astra.
> Signat cuncta manu: loquiturque Polymnia gestu
> Mentis Apollineae vis has movet undique musas:
> In medio residens complectitur omnia Phoebus.

For certain of Sp.'s Muses these lines offer sufficient explanation, to wit: Melpomene (*T.M.* 115–74; *S.C.* Nov. 19, 52; *Mui.* 10, 413; cf. E.K. on Nov. 52), Thalia (*T.M.* 175–234), Euterpe (*T.M.* 235–92), who becomes the Muse of the pastoral;

Polyhymnia (*T.M.* 541–94), who presides over rhetoric and whose complaint is chiefly a criticism of literary expression (cf. E.K. on April 100). In his treatment of the other Muses, Sp. goes further than what these lines offer. Terpsichore (*T.M.* 301–60) has little to do with the dance but seems to be thought of rather generally as a patroness of letters (cf. especially *T.M.* 310,f.). Fulgentius (1.15) describes her as "delectans instructione," and this is taken over by Bocc., 11.2; cf. Renwick, *Compl.*, p. 212. Erato (*T.M.* 361–420) presides over love poetry; cf. *Phaedrus* 259D (S) and Linocier, *Mythologiae Musarum*, cap. vii,[8] who says that her name means love, deriving it from the Greek. Urania (*T.M.* 481–534) is something more than the Muse of astronomy, a giver of the highest knowledge of the universe and of man; cf. Plutarch, *Quaest. Conv.* 9.14.7; *Phaedrus, loc. cit.*, where Urania is patroness of philosophers and one of those "Muses who are chiefly concerned with heaven and thought divine as well as human."

Clio and Calliope are reserved for treatment together. In *T.M.* their complaints make them quite similar. Calliope presides over the brave deeds to which she incites men by the hope of praise; hence she is called "the nurse of virtue . . . and golden trumpet of eternity" (451–8). Clio is also the giver of fame who registers "all noble feats" and sounds them "in trump of gold" (77–8). The similarity in the functions of these two Muses arises partly from the undiscriminating way in which they are used throughout classical poetry. It also reflects the Renaissance doctrine that epic poetry and history are alike in their aim to glorify noble deeds and so inspire virtuous imitation. The resulting ambiguity makes it difficult to decide which of the two Sp. had in mind as the Muse of *F.Q.* However, several considerations make it fairly certain that Clio was intended. (a) *F.Q.* contains four formal invocations to the Muse (1.Pr.1–2; 1.11.5–7; 3.3.4; 4.11.10). She is named only once, at 3.3.4, where she is called Clio; but in all four passages there is the same conception of her province. She is the keeper of "the antique rolles" (1.Pr.2), "the great volume of eternity" (3.3.4), "the records of antiquity" (4.11.10), in which "Knights and Ladies gentle deeds" (1.Pr.1) and heroes' warlike deeds are inscribed; and she is "the nourse of time and everlasting fame" (1.11.5), because she immortalizes such noble deeds with everlasting glory and praise. Such a conception of Clio was traditional before Sp. and appears in two of his most likely sources, Bocc., 11.2, and Linocier, *op. cit.*, cap. ii, who interpret her name as meaning glory or fame and go on to say that, as such, she not only enshrines the noble deeds of history, but inspires great acts by her appeal to man's love of fame.[9] (b) In the Letter to Raleigh Sp. calls his poem "an historicall fiction" and refers to former epic poets as "historical." Clio is the appropriate patroness of an epic so conceived. (c) In the pseudo-Vergilian epigram quoted above and in *T.M.* 53, Clio is the eldest of the Muses. At 1.Pr.2 the Muse invoked

---

[8] This work was appended to the 1583 edition of N.C. and to most subsequent editions.

[9] The passages in Bocc. and Linocier, with other illustrative material, are collected by Mrs. Bennett, "Spenser's Muse," *JEGP*, 31.200–219. Her work tends to corroborate rather than change conclusions I had reached before it appeared. I am indebted to her here and at one point noted below. For an argument in favor of Calliope as Sp.'s chief muse, see F. M. Padelford, "The Muse of *The Faerie Queene*," *SP*, 27.111–124.

is "holy virgin, chiefe of nyne." While one cannot say that, in the tradition before Sp., all these points would apply only to Clio and not to Calliope, it seems reasonably probable, even taking the internal evidence alone, that Clio is Sp.'s chief Muse.

If this is so, then the troublesome line, "Meanwhile, O Clio, lend Calliope thy quill" (7.6.37), means that Clio is to step aside and let Calliope tell the story of Faunus and Molanna, which is to be in a lighter, less grandly epic vein ("Mongst these sterne stounds to mingle soft delights"). When it is over, the "greater Muse" (Clio) recalls him from "woods and pleasing forrests . . . in bigger noates to sing" of the epic doings of Mutability (7.1.1). That Calliope was, in Sp.'s mind, the more appropriate patroness of the lighter, more fanciful sort of poetry which he is writing in 7.6.38,f. is suggested by the fact that she and not Clio is mentioned in *S.C.* (April 100–108, June 57–61) and by the tradition that she presides over poetical invention and that her name means "of sweet voice" (Bocc. *loc. cit.*, Linocier, *op. cit.* cap. x).[10]

Something of what Sp. saw in Clio is extended to his conception of the Muses in general. The idea that the Muses, as sources of poetic inspiration, have in their keeping all the matter of poetry, figuratively thought of as history, is implicit in most of his references to them and is best seen in 6.Pr.2–3. It is, of course, paralleled in the classics; cf. especially *Aen.* 9.525–8 and *Theb.* 10.628–31, where the figure of the records, or rolls, appears. The idea that poetic immortality is the gift of the Muses in general appears at *R.T.* 393–9, 402; *Ded. Son.* 4. In accord with the principle that high poetry must be learned, the Muses are "learned sisters (*Epith.* 1), "learned daughters" (2.10.3), "ornaments of light" (*M.H.T.* 762), "ladies of learning" (E.K. on April 42; cf. gloss on April 41), who "the keeping have of learnings threasures" (6.Pr.2). Van Winkle, p. 76, cites *Met.* 5.255; *Fasti* 6.811; *Tristia* 2.13; cf. also Vergil, *Catalepton* 9.2. The idea behind this loomed large in Renaissance poetic and its importance to Sp. is shown by the nature of the Muses' complaints against Ignorance and Barbarism in *T.M.*

References to the Muses' crown of bays occur at *S.C.* April 104, Nov. 146; *CCCHA* 414; cf. Linocier, *op. cit.*: the laurel is sacred to the Muses "certe quia laurus est semper virens, hocque pacto opera Musarum sint semper virida." References to the music of the Muses, to Sp. a very real thing, are at *S.C.* April 100,f., June 29; *T.M.* 6; *V.P.* 4; 1.10.54; 1.11.7. See also *Graces, Heliades, Helicon, Mermaids, Naiads.*

MUTABILITY 7.6.1,f.

The Titaness Mutability is Sp.'s own embodiment, not only of the forces of change and decay which he felt so keenly, but also of those qualities of false pride and rebellious ambition which were a part of his conception of the Titans, from whom he derives her (7.6.2, 27). Thus he speaks of her as "Proud Change" (7.6. arg.), of her "bold presumption" (7.6.2), her "pride and impudence" (7.6.25), her "hot bold

---

10 Cf. Bennett, *op. cit.* 202–3, 208, for further illustrative quotations. Cf. E.K. on April 100.

emprise" (7.6.22). See *Titans*. Sp. may have found a suggestive connecting link in N.C.'s idea (6.20) that the myth of the Titans' rebellion and fall represents "elementorum mutationes." The reference to "the ever-whirling *wheele* Of Change, the which all mortal things doth sway" (7.6.1) suggests that, to some extent, Sp. is creating his Titaness on the pattern of the classical and medieval goddess Fortuna; see *Fortune*. A consideration of N.C.'s chapter on Fortuna (4.9) lends weight to this supposition, for his description of that goddess corresponds at many points with Sp.'s Mutability: She is said by Orpheus to have been born of blood (cf. 7.6.20; cf. *Earth*). N.C. goes on to describe her as "stultam" and "temerariam" and says that to her "penes quam omnes humanae vitae *mutationes* . . . arbitrium esse creditur . . . . Vitam omnium mortalium Fortunae ludum esse crediderint" (cf. 7.6.1.5). Finally, N.C. offers the information, from what source does not appear, that at one time Fortuna, like Mutability, almost succeeded in ousting Jove from his throne: "Haec eadem [Fortuna] tantum existimationis, tantumque imperium ab Homeri temporibus accepit, ut Iupiter de coelo ab ea prope fuerit detrusus, omnemque rerum administrationem et sceptrum ipsum e manibus illa Iovis prope extorserit. . . ."

MYRRHA 3.2.41; 3.7.26; 4.7.22.

Sp. may have known Ovid's account of Myrrha, *Met.* 10.312, f. He alludes twice to her flight from her father (3.7.26; 4.7.22), which is a part of Ovid's story. The allusion at 3.2.41 follows *Ciris* 238–40; cf. Hughes, p. 351.

NAIADS *V.G.* 25–6; 1.6.18.

At *V.G.* 25–6, translating *Culex* 18–19, Sp. addresses the Naiads as "ye sisters which the glory be Of the Pierian streames." The close connection of both Naiads and Muses with springs would tend to draw them together, as here. Cf. *Ecl.* 10.10.– 12, where they are identified. At 1.6.18 there is bare mention of "the troop of light-foot Naiades." At *V.G.* 179 Sp. renders "Naiadum coetu" (*Culex* 117) as "many fairies." See *Nymphs*.

NAIS 7.7.40. See *Philyra*.

NARCISSUS *V.G.* 679; 3.2.44; 3.6.45; *Am.* 35.

Narcissus appears as the flower into which his love changed him at 3.6.45 and *V.G.* 679, which slightly elaborates *Culex* 408–9. Sp. makes a skillful transfer from the character of Narcissus to his flower in the line, "Foolish Narcisse, that likes the watry shore" (3.6.45). On the use of Narcissus at *Am.* 35 Renwick, *Daph.*, p. 200, cites Ronsard, *Amours* 1.157. The phrase, "so plenty makes me poor," translates *Met.* 3.466. Ovid tells the story (*Met.* 3.402, f.) with emphasis on Narcissus' loving a shadow and "thinking that substance which is only a shade." So, when he finds that his beloved is himself, he exclaims, "inopem me copia fecit." This phrase Sp. had used as the emblem for *S.C.* Sept.; see E.K.'s gloss. The same idea leads Sp. to make Britomart compare herself, who "feeds on shadows," to "Cephisus foolish chyld" (3.2.44). Thus, for Sp., Narcissus was not so much one who loved himself as one who was deluded and starved by shadows.

NATURE

Sp.'s conception of Nature as a goddess is a part of a long tradition.[11] He conceived of her primarily as the creator, nurse, and orderer of life (cf. *S.C.* Nov. 123; *T.M.* 499–502; 1.11.47; 2.2.6; 2.6.15, 16; 2.12.23; 3.6.30; 4.6.24; 4.9.16; 4.10.21; *Daph.* 337). The frequent references to "Dame Nature" are a part of this conception. Nature's part in the creation of the world may be gathered from *T.M.* 499–502, which follows *Met.* 1.21,f. A corollary to the idea of Nature as the nurse and orderer of life is the antithesis of Nature and Art, of which Sp. is fond (cf. 3.6.30; 3.6.44; 6.10.5 and 2.12.46, 48, 50); cf. *Met.* 3.158–9.

Definitely personified as a character in the action, Nature plays her most important rôle in *Mut.* She is not only the arbiter of Mutability's claims; she is throughout the representative of law and order, without which, in Sp.'s mind, life could not go on. Mutability has upset "all which Nature had established first In good estate, and in meet order ranged." (7.6.5). Nature's "sergeant" is called Order (7.7.4). The description of her at 7.7.5–13 is intentionally vague and mysterious, but seems to show some points of indebtedness to earlier treatments of the goddess. From Alanus de Insulis, *De Planctu Naturae*, Prose 1, he seems to have taken a suggestion for comparing her face to a lion. Alanus says that one of the jewels in Natura's crown was like a lion. Otherwise the two descriptions are quite different.[12] Sp. seems to be indebted to Chaucer for the comparison of Nature with the splendor of the sun (cf. *P.F.* 299–301) and for the point that she is on a hill covered with trees and flowers (cf. *P.F.* 302). For the veil which covers Nature and suggests that she is of ambiguous sex, Sp. probably used Plutarch's description of the statue of Isis (*De Iside*, chap. 9), which he also used at 4.10.40. 7.7.13 gives something of her inner qualities. She is "great grandmother of all creatures bred . . . ever young yet full of eld" and "still mooving, yet unmoved from her sted." Upton compares Boethius, *De. Cons. Phil.* 3, metre 9, on the God of Nature, "Stabulisque manens, das cuncta moveri." The Orphic Hymn to Natura and Alanus provide illustrative parallels to the matter of this passage and to Sp.'s larger conception of Nature as described above. "Orpheus" addresses her as "Nature, the parent of all . . . 'daedale' mother, . . . first born, . . . without end, . . . father and mother of all things (cf. 7.7.5.6), . . . nurse, . . . eternal and ever moving (cf. 7.7.13.3.)." Alanus metre 4 is similar and may be based partly on "Orpheus": "O offspring of God, creator of all things, . . . bond and firm chain of the universe, order, . . . pattern of the world, . . . at whose nod the world grows young, the forest is curled with leafy

---

[11] For very helpful studies of the tradition of Natura in classical and medieval literature, see E. C. Knowlton, "The Goddess Natura in Early Periods," *JEGP*, 19.224, f.; "Nature in Middle English," *JEGP*, 20.186, f.; "Nature in Old French," *MP*, 20.309, f.
[12] But see E. Greenlaw, "Some Old Religious Cults in Spenser," *SP*, 20.216–43.

locks and, clothed in its tunic of blossoms, the earth exults" (cf. 7.7.10). Finally, the idea that Nature is the "vicegerent of God the creator," found in Alanus Prose 3, whence it passes into *The Romance of the Rose* 16970 and Chaucer, *Physician's Tale* C 19–21, is implicit in the rôle which Nature plays in *Mut.* and explains the transition at the end from Nature to the God of Sabbaoth.

NECTAR *S.C.* Nov. 195; *T.M.* 218; *R.T.* 399; 3.1.36; 3.4.40; 3.6.18; 3.11.2; *Am.* 39; *H.L.* 25–6, 282; *H.B.* 249.

At Nov. 195; *R.T.* 399; *H.L.* 282 Sp. uses nectar and ambrosia in the most common classical way, as the drink and food of the gods; cf. *Od.* 5.199, 9.359; *Theog.* 640, 796. 3.6.18, where Diana's hair is described as "with sweet ambrosia all besprinkled light," is rather close to *Aen.* 1.403, where Venus, in the guise of Diana, has "ambrosiae comae." At *Am.* 39 and *H.L.* 26 "ambrosial" is used loosely, somewhat as in the Vergilian phrase just quoted. At 3.4.40 nectar is used as a medicine. Nectar and ambrosia appear as balms at *Il.* 19.38–9, 357–9, and ambrosia also at *Il.* 16.670 and *Aen.* 12.419. 3.1.36 may be taken as an extension of the same idea. The association of nectar with love here is found also at 3.11.2 and *H.B.* 249. From this it is not a great step to the idea that nectar is sprinkled on the sweet verse of Raleigh's *Cynthia* (3.Pr.4) and flows from the pen of the "gentle spirit" of *T.M.* 218.

NELEUS 4.11.14. See *Sea-Gods.*

NEMEAN LION *Mui.* 71–2; 2.5.31; 5.Pr.6; 7.7.36; *Daph.* 166.

Mui. 71–2 refers to "Alcides with the lyons skin, When the Naemean conquest he did win." Sp. seems somewhat vague as to just when he acquired his lion's skin. In N.C. 7.1 it is just after "the Naemean conquest." Classical allusions to the myth are scanty. On 2.5.31 see *Hercules*; on 5.Pr.6; 7.7.36; *Daph.* 166 see "Leo" under *Zodiac.*

NEMERTEA 4.11.51. See *Nereids.*

NEMESIS *Mui.* 2.

Sp. is parodying the conventional way of beginning an epic and is probably thinking particularly of the opening lines of *Il.* His introduction of Nemesis is, of course, original, but he uses her in her classical character; cf. Ovid, who associates her with wrath (*Met.* 14.694) and with vengeance (*Tristia* 8.9). Cf. *Theog.* 223, "Deadly Night bore Nemesis, an affliction to mortal men."

NEPENTHE 4.3.42–43.

Cambina brings the drink which banishes grief and rage and gives eternal happiness. Cf. *Od.* 4.220.f. (Upton). Sp. may have been developing the etymology. Cf. also Theophrastus, *History of Plants* 9.15.1, where he quotes *Od. loc. cit.* and says "Among these [drugs] was *nepenthes*, the famous drug which cures sorrows and passion so that it causes forgetfulness and indifference to ills."

NEPTUNE

References to Neptune in his common classical character as god of the sea are numerous (*S.C.* Feb. 33; *R.R.* 13; 1.3.32; 1.11.54; 2.12.22; 3.4.10; 4.12.30; 7.7.26). His name is also used for the sea itself (3.4.32; 3.4.42), following classical usage; cf. *Geo.* 4.29; Moschus 2.115,f. At 4.12.1–2, where Sp. speaks of "the seas abundant progeny" and its fruitfulness, he probably has N.C. 2.8 in mind: "Ingens filiorum Neptuni numerus praeterea, quid nisi maris fertilitas est?" 3.11.40–41 gives a vivid picture of Neptune coming over the sea; it is based on *Aen.* 5.817–21, but shows considerable elaboration. Neptune's trident is mentioned here and at *Mui.* 313 and 4.11.11. Especially with the last passage cf. N.C. *loc. cit.*, "Tridens vero quem habet Neptunus pro sceptro, triplicem illius ostendit potestatem, quod habet facultatem scilicet tollendi aequoris et placandi et servandi." *Mui.* 313–20 describes the contest of Minerva and Neptune for dominion over Athens. Neptune "strikes the rockes with his three-forked mace; Whenceforth issues a warlike steed in sight." Sp. is following *Met.* 6.75–7 closely. In line 77 his text must have read "ferum" where modern editions have "fretum." Micyllus' note on the line (Burmann 2.384–5), or *Geo.* 1.12–14, or Bocc. 5.48 would have told him that by "ferum" a "warlike steed" was meant. When Britomart vows a votive tablet to Neptune (3.4.10) if Aeolus will see her ship to the "port of her intent," she is making use of a classical custom which is treated mostly notably by Horace, *Odes* 1.5.13,f. On 3.8.30 see *Proteus*. On 3.11.42.2–4; 4.9.23 see *Arne;* on 3.11.41–42 see *Bisaltis, Iphimedia, Medusa, Melantho;* on 1.5.38 see *Theseus;* on 4.11.12–16 see *Sea-Gods* and *Founders of Nations*.

NEREIDS 4.11.48–53.6.

In these stanzas Sp. seems to be following N.C. 8.6, p. 833–5, in the main. St. 50.4–6, on Cymodoce, and the epithets of Glauconome and Alimeda are from *Theog.* 252–6. Mrs. Bennett shows ("Spenser's Hesiod," *Am. Jour. of Philol.*, 52.176–81) that Sp. probably used the Latin translation of *Theog.* by Boninus Mombritius for his characterization of Galathea, Eunica, Glauce, Galene, Erato, Polynome, and Agave. The lines on Cymodoce, which she assigns to the Latin, are as close to the Greek. In N.C. the Nereids are daughters of Nereus and Doris (cf. st. 48.3–5). He quotes Horace, *Odes* 3.28.10, to the effect that they have green hair (cf. st. 48.2). He next quotes *Il.* 18. 39–49, which Sp. does not seem to have used, and then gives a list of 49 of the 50 names found in *Theog.* 240–64. He omits Thoe, changes Polynoe to Polynome, and has Spio, Eucrate, and Thalia for Hesiod's Speio, Eucrante, and Halia. Sp. follows N.C. in all these omissions and changes and in his order is closer to N.C. than to Hesiod. Sp. differs from N.C.'s list only in omitting Cymatolege, in which he may follow Mombritius, who also leaves out Thoe, and he adds two names not found elsewhere, Phao and Poris.

Sp. has taken the names of the Nereids as self-descriptive and so as representing the multitudinous aspects of the sea. He has not lost this opportunity to indulge his bent for etymology. He has gone far beyond his predecessors in attaching to the names epithets which bring out their meaning. I list the cases in which this etymologizing, independent of sources, seems clearly discernible: "swift Proto" (προωθέω); "milde Eucrate" (εὐ-κρατέω); "joyous Thalia (θάλεια); "light foote Cymothoe" (κῦμο-θοή); "sweete Melite" (μελιτόεις); "Phao lilly white" (φάω); "wise Protomedaea" (πρωτο-μήδομαι); "speedy Hippothoe" (θοή); "Pronaea sage" (πρόνοη, ,πρόνοια); "Eione well in age" (perhaps thinking of αἰών); "Liagore, much praisd for wise behests" (λεῖος, ἀγορεύω); "Themiste juste" (θεμιστή); "Nemertea, learned well to rule her lust" (νημερτής). On 4.11.52 see Nereis.

NEREIS V.G. 567.

With slight expansion, this translates Culex 345–6. Sp. probably uses the name here generically for a Nereid (cf. "Nais," 7.7.40). The idea that the Nereids controlled the waves (cf. 4.11.52) and guided ships is found also at Ap. Rh. 4.930–38; Silvae 3.213,f., and N.C. 8.6, where he says, "the Nereids have control over the arts and counsels of sea-faring."

NEREUS V.G. 492; V.B. 13; 1.3.31; 3.4.19,f.; 4.11.18–19; 4.11.48, 52.

On 4.11.18–19, the most extended characterization of Nereus, S. cites Theog. 233–36 and Horace, Odes 1.15.1–8. It appears, however, that Sp. found these two passages quoted, with his other material, in N.C. 8.6, p. 832. Sp. follows N.C.'s quotations and comments in the same order: first the lines from Hesiod, then N.C.'s statement that Nereus was a famous soothsayer, and then the two stanzas from Horace. He does not include anything not in N.C. His final bit of characterization (4.11.19.8–9) comes, not from the classical sources, but from a statement by N.C. on the same page as the quotations: "Hunc [Nereus] mari praeesse, et in mari habitare solitum, delectari choris puellarum," and, quoting Orpheus, "laetate puellis Formosisque choris, Nereu, ... "

Like Thetis, Tethys, and Neptune, Nereus is conceived as immanent in the sea and his name is often synonymous with it. So at 1.3.31 and V.B. 13, where Nereus is not in the French original, Songe 13; cf. Ecl. 6.35; Aen. 10.764; Met. 1.187. V.G. 492 expands Culex 300. On 3.4.19 see Cymodoce; on 4.11.48, 52 see Nereids.

NESAEA, NESO 4.11.49, 50. See Nereids.

NESTOR 2.9.48, 57.

Sp. remembers him for his wisdom, his eloquence, and his age. 2.9.48 may represent a memory of Met. 12.187–8, but line 5 seems clearly to echo Il. 1.250–52. The idea that by Nestor's advice Troy fell, not Homeric, may come from Dares, De Excidio Troiae Historia, cap. 3.

NICTILIUS V.G. 173. See Bacchus.

NIGHT *T.M.* 263; *V.G.* 313; 1.4.44; 1.5.20, f.; 1.7.2; 1.11.49; 2.4.41; 3.4.55,f.; 3.5.22; 3.10.16; 5.10.10; 7.7.44–45; *Epith.* 98–9, 315–331.

Night is used most elaborately at 1.5.20,f. From *Met.* 14.403–5, where Circe summons Night to her aid, may have come a suggestion for introducing her here as a helper to Duessa; but it seems likely that a large share of the material is from N.C. 3.12. Sp.'s night is "most auncient grandmother of all, . . . begot in Daemogorgon's hall," which is Chaos. N.C. says, "She is called most ancient because she was born of Chaos, for she lived before the world was digested into order (cf. st. 22.6). Therefore rightly Orpheus in his hymns calls her the mother of gods and men (cf. st. 22.2–3)." In accord with this, she is the wife of Erebus (2.4.41; 3.4.55); see *Erebus*. She is "mother of Falsehood" and so of Duessa (1.5.27); cf. *Theog.* 224; Bocc. 1.21, and N.C. 3.12, where Deceit or Fraud is a child of Night. 1.5.20 also gives the fullest description of Night's physical appearance. Here Sp. follows N.C.'s order: the black mantle (which appears also at 1.11.49; 7.7.44; *Epith.* 321; cf. Euripides, *Ion* 1150, quoted by N.C.), the chariot (cf. *Aen.* 5.721, quoted by N.C.), the horses (which appear also at 7.7.44, where Sp. may be thinking of the Moon's black and white horses; see *Diana*). To these properties Sp. adds, at 7.7.44, "a mace, On top whereof the moon and stars were pight." A suggestion for this may have come from Claudian, *R.P.* 2.363, where Night is "clad in starry raiment." *Epith.* 319 adds a mention of Night's wing; cf. *Aen.* 8.369, quoted by N.C. The natural and habitual home of Night is Hades, which, for Sp., is in a general way identified with Chaos (1.5.20,f.; 3.4.55; *V.G.* 313; 3.5.22; 5.10.10). At 1.5.30 Night's approach makes the dogs bay; cf. *Aen.* 6.257–8, where the dogs howl at the approach of Hecate. Arthur's invocation to Night (3.4.55,f.) adds further elements to the picture. St. 56–4–8 is reminiscent of Euripides, *Orestes* 176,f., quoted by N.C., *loc. cit.* In N.C., as at st. 57.5–6, Night is the giver of dreams. Sp.'s list (st. 58) of the evil things which are hidden under Night's "mantle black" corresponds roughly to N.C.'s list of the offspring of Night (based on Cicero, *Nat. Deor.* 3.17 and *Theog.* 211,f.; cf. Claudian, *In Rufinum* 1.28,f.): "Dolus, Metus, Labor, Fatum, Mors, Tenebrae, Miseria, Fraus, etc."[13] No explanation appears for the statement at *Epith.* 330–1 that Jove and Night begot Majesty. A goddess Majesty, daughter of Honor and Reverence, is mentioned by Ovid, *Fasti* 5.23–5 and Bocc., 3.12. On 7.7.45 and *Epith.* 98–9 see *Hours*.

NIOBE *S.C.* April 86; 4.7.30; 5.10.7.

In all these references, the killing of Niobe's children by Diana and Apollo, as a result of her boasting, is uppermost in Sp.'s mind. E.K.'s gloss on April 86 tells the story, following *Met.* 6.146,f., which is probably the source for Sp.'s other allusions to the myth. At 5.10.7 Sp. seems to adapt *Met.* 6.152–55 to fit Belge, with whom Niobe is compared.

---

[13] Lemmi, p. 275, cites this passage in N.C. in connection with 1.5.20–44, but does not note the other parallels.

NUMA 2.10.39, 42. See *Aegerie*.

NYMPHS

Sp. knows three classes of Nymphs: Dryads or Hamadryads, Naiads, and Nereids (see under these names). Thus at *Epith*. 37-9 he calls upon the nymphs of rivers, of forests, and of the sea; cf. Servius, *ad Aen*. 1.500. It is the association of Nymphs with water that Sp. develops most fully. When, at 4.11.52, he speaks of the nymphs that "all mankind do nourish with their waters clere.", he is following a tradition most fully discussed by N.C., 5.12[14], to the effect that the nymphs represent the nature of water and thereby a cosmic generative force. Sp. has made particular use of this idea, combined with the idea of the sun as a generative force, in the story of Chrysogone (3.6.4-10). He may have taken a suggestion from N.C. 10, p. 1034, "Cum enim Nymphae materia sunt in rebus naturalibus, illae formam recipiunt ac fovent: est enim Dionysus virtus Solis generationi conferens, quae vicem maris obtinet in operibus naturae." The association of nymphs with springs and fountains is present at *S.C.* April 37 and 2.1.55 (cf. E.K. on April 120). The idyllic picture at *V.B.* 12 of nymphs about a spring, routed by satyrs, is translated from *Songe* 12 (cf. *V.P.* 4). Nymphs and Muses, through their association with fountains, have been partially identified (*V.G.* 25-6; cf. *Daph*. 314; *V.P.* 4; see *Naiads*). Bocc., 7.14, says, "Sunt [Nymphae] enim fontes, fluviorum continuum nutrimentum. Ex his enim numerantur novem, quibus Castalius fons dicatus . . . Musae vocantur." At 2.2.7,f. Sp. creates his own myth of the nymph of the fountain to explain the peculiar properties of the water; see *Faunus*. At 1.7.4 he makes up the story of the nymph who fell out of Diana's favor because of her laziness, this time working on the idea of the fountain which takes away energy, which appears at *Met*. 15.319-21.

Presenting a somewhat different aspect, the nymphs appear frequently as the representatives of chastity (1.7.5; 1.12.7; 2.3.31; 3.6.19, 23; 4.7.23; 5.8.43; 7.6.39; 7.6.42, 45, 51). It is chiefly their association with Diana, as in all these references, that is responsible for this. In accord with this idea of nymphs, Sp. translates "nymphe" (*Songe* 10.1) as "virgin" (*V.B.* 10.1), and Belphoebe is brought up "in perfect maydenhed" by a nymph (3.6.28). The association of nymphs with Venus (*Mui*. 115,f.) has no special significance and nymphs following Pan (*S.C.* Dec. 47) are common enough in the pastoral (cf. *Geo.* 2.494 and see *Silvanus*).

Sp.'s nymphs have in many places become completely naturalized and are quite at home with English fairies (cf. *S.C.* May 33, June 26; *T.M.* 31; 6.10.7; E.K. on April 120). Thus, at *V.G.* 146, Sp. translated "Hamadryadum" (*Culex* 95) as "country nymphs" and at *V.G.*179, "Naiadum" (*Culex* 117) as "fairies"[15]. Tristram lives in the woods among the nymphs (6.2.25) and the country girls about Kilcolman are "ye nymphes of Mulla" (*Epith.* 57).

---

[14] "Illas igitur vires, ex quibus universa generatio consistit, intra aquarum naturam Nymphas antiqui appelarunt . . . Cum ex his viribus omnia oriuntur, quae primum videbantur se in flumina diffundere, fluviorum matres dictae sunt (cf. 7.7.26), et per hos denique *universae generationis parentes* sunt vocatae, hinc fructiferae merito, *hinc homines et animalia omnia nutrire*."

[15] The frequent equation of nymphs and fairies before Sp. is discussed by Ritson in Hazlitt's *Fairy Tales, Legends and Romances Illustrating Shakespeare*, pp. 9, f. Cf. Gower, *Con. Am.* 1.2315, f.; Chaucer, *Merchant's Tale* E2227.

OCEAN 2.12.65; 4.11.18, 48, 52; 6.Pr.7; 6.10.22.

Ocean and "his dame old Tethys" are, in Sp.'s mind, symbols of beginning and generation. At 4.11.18 he is the father of "all the rest . . . which afterward both sea and land possest." He is the father of the sea-nymphs (4.11.52) and, in particular, of Doris (4.11.48) and Eurynome (6.10.22). At 6.Pr.7 Sp.traces all virtue from Elizabeth, even as "from the ocean all rivers spring And tribute back repay as to their king." The idea of the fruitfulness of the ocean appears most strikingly at 2.12.65 and 4.12.1–2, where it is related to the myth of Venus' birth; cf. *Neptune*. A passage from N.C. (8.1) will illustrate the interpretation of Oceanus which Sp. inherited and used: "Oceanus, qui fluviorum et animantium omnium et Deorum pater vocatus est ab antiquis, . . . quippe cum omnia priusquam oriantur aut intercidant, indigeant humore: sine quo nihil neque corrumpi potest, neque gigni."

OEDIPUS *V.G.* Ded. 5; 5.11.25.

Both references are to Oedipus' reading the riddle of the Sphinx; cf. *Sphinx*. At 5.11.25 he is called "the Theban knight, The father of that fatall progeny," Eteocles and Polyneices.

OENONE 3.9.36; 6.9.36. See *Paris*.

OGYGES 4.11.15. See *Founders of Nations*.

OLYMPUS *R.R.* 2; 3.7.41.

In both passages Sp. confuses Olympus with Olympia. At 3.7.41 he speaks of chariot races as taking place on Mount Olympus. Upton notes the same mistake in Sidney's *Defense of Poesy* (see ed. Cook, p. 30). The error might have come from N.C., 5.1, who, in a very full account of the Olympic Games, does not mention Olympia as a separate place and, in his Greek quotations, translates Ὀλυμπιακὸν ἀγῶνα as "certamina Olympi" and Ὀλύμπια as "Olympus." The line "Joves great image in Olympus placed" (*R.R.* 2), following *Ant. Rome* 2.6, "De son grand Juppiter l'image Olympienne," would be a natural translation for one who did not know Olympia as a place separate from Olympus.

OPS 7.7.26.

Ops as "rule and sovranty . . . of the earth." S. cites Macrobius, *Saturnalia* 1.10.20. Bocc. 3.2, largely dependent on Macrobius, would be more accessible to Sp. Bocc. identifies her with Cybele, Berecynthia, and Rhea, as "deorum Mater," presiding over the earth and representing its powers. "Sceptrum autem quod manibus defert, regna, divitias, et potentiam imperantium super terra monstrabat."

ORCUS 2.12.41; 6.12.26.

At 2.12.41 Sp. uses Orcus as a name for Pluto. It is so used in Horace, *Odes* 2.3.24; *Met.* 14.116–7. At 6.12.26 Orcus is Hades itself. The Blatant Beast's mouth is "like the mouth of Orcus griesly grim." Cf. *Aen.* 6.273, "in faucibus Orci"; Lucan 6.714.

ORESTES 4.10.27.

Orestes and Pylades appear as famous friends, grouped, as here, with Theseus and Pirithous, at *Theb.* 1.476–7 and Claudian, *In Rufinum* 1.107–8. With Sp.'s list of friends as a whole, cf. Lyly, *Euphues* (ed. Croll and Clemens, p. 30), "Damon to his Pythias, Pylades to his Orestes, Titus to his Gysippus, Theseus to his Pirithous, Scipio to his Laelius will never be found more faithful than Euphues to his Philautas."

ORGOGLIO See *Giants*.

ORION 1.3.31; 2.2.46; 4.11.13; 7.7.39.

Orion appears in all these passages as a giant and mighty hunter and at the same time as a constellation. The version of his death given at 7.7.39 does not agree exactly with any of the classical versions and probably follows N.C. 8.22: "Dianae quoque, cum una venaretur, aiunt vim inferre voluisse, quare illius iussu occisum fuisse, ut in his testatur Euphorion, 'Dea irata scorpium e terra excitavit, qui illius talum percutiens interemit.' " With 2.2.46 cf. *Ciris* 535 and N.C. *loc. cit.*, "Cum vero Orion oppositum habeat scorpionem, videtur semper illum fugere ex eodem hemisphaerio." At 4.11.13 "Orion that doth tempests still portend" recalls Vergil's "nimbosus Orion," *Aen.* 1.535. At 1.3.31 Sirius, the dog star, is identified with Orion's hound; so Hygin., *P.A.* 2.35 (S). Sirius appears also at *S.C.* July 22; *M.H.T* 5; *R.R.* 26 in a character entirely classical; cf. *Geo.* 4.425; *Aen.* 3.141; Horace, *Odes* 3.13.9–10; *Fasti* 4.939–40.

ORPHEUS *S.C.* Oct. 29; *V.G.* 180, 433–80; *R.T.* 332, 390–2, 593–6, 607; *R.R.* 25; 4.2.1; 4.10.58; *Am.* 44; *Epith.* 16; *H.L.* 234–5.

A rather full version of the Orpheus and Eurydice story is given at *V.G.* 433–80, and Sp. may have drawn on this passage for some of his other references to the myth. He follows *Culex* 268–96 with some independence. He certainly knew the beautiful version at *Geo.* 4. 453–529 and the more circumstantial one at *Met.* 10.1,f. His other references to the story serve to show what aspects of it impressed him: the taming of Cerberus (*S.C.* Oct. 29); how Orpheus won back his bride through the help of the Muses (*R.T.* 390–2); how the power of love made him "daring to provoke the ire of damned fiends" (*H.L.* 234–5). It was Orpheus the poet who meant most to Sp. By the power of his music he calmed the civil strife of the Argonauts (4.2.1; *Am.* 44; cf. Ap. Rh. 1.492,f.; N.C. 7.14). At *R.T.* 603–9 the story of Orpheus' harp is adapted to fit Sidney (cf. *Met.* 11.50–2), and Sidney is said to be with Orpheus and Linus in the Elysian Fields (*R.T.* 332–3; see *Linus*). On the unusual reference at *Epith.* 16 to Orpheus singing his own epithalamium, Van Winkle cites Claudian, *Epist. ad Serenam* 1–6. Sp. might have caught the idea from *Met.* 10.1–3, "Hymen . . . summoned by the voice of Orpheus, though all in vain."

ORSILOCHUS 3.4.2. See *Camilla*.

ORTHRUS 5.10.10.

Sp. follows *Theog.* 309 in making Orthrus the offspring of Typhaon and Echidna.
For the rest he is probably indebted to N.C. 6.1; see *Geryon*.

OSIRIS 5.7.2,f. See *Isis*.

OSSA 2.10.3. See *Giants*.

OTHOS *V.G.* 373–6.

Sp. is translating *Culex* 234–6. Othos, a Giant, sits in Hades, bound with serpents,
with his brother Ephialtes, "which once assai'd to burn this world so wide." For
this last line Sp. must have had before him Bembo's reading "incendere" for "in-
scendere" at *Culex* 236 (see Plésent, p. 178; Emerson, p. 108). The result is a version
of the myth which differs from that given at *Od.* 11.305,f. or *Aen.* 6.582–4.

PACTOLUS *V.G.* 12; 4.6.20; 4.11.20.

The simile at 4.6.20 suggests that Sp. had in mind the description of Pactolus at
Met. 11.142–5. *V.B.* 12, "the golden grayle that bright Pactolus washeth," translates *Songe* 12. "Pactolus, glistering with his golden flood "(4.11.20) comes to the
marriage of the Thames and the Medway.

PAEON 3.4.41.

This rather vague figure, scantily represented in classical literature (cf. *Od.* 4.232)
was identified, sometimes with Apollo, sometimes with Aesculapius. Making him
the son of Apollo, Sp. may be identifying him with Aesculapius. On the story of
Paeon's birth see *Liagore*.

PAIN 2.7.21. See *Hades*.

PALAEMON 4.11.13; 5.8.47. See *Ino, Sea-Gods*.

PALES *V.G.* 28–32, 116.

In both passages Pales appears in her traditional character as the Latin goddess of
agriculture and fertility; cf. *Fasti* 4.722–4 (S); *Ecl.* 5.35; *Geo.* 3.1, 294. In each case
Sp. is translating *Culex* (20–22, 77) closely.

PALICI *T.M.* 13–18.

There is no precedent in classic myth for this passage. Perhaps, as S. suggests,
Sp. confused the nymph Thalia, proper mother of the Palici (Servius, *ad Aen.* 9.581;
Macrobius, *Saturnalia* 5.19.16,f.) with the muse Thalia, and that muse with Calli-
ope, who, as Renwick notices (*Compl.*, p. 206) had lamented her son Orpheus.

PALLAS *Mui.* 262, 301, 346. See *Minerva.*

PAN *S.C.* Jan. 17, 67; April 50,f., 91,f.; May 54, 111; June 30, 68; July 49, 144, 179; Sept. 96; Nov. 8, 10; Dec. 7–12, 50; 2.9.40.

In keeping with pastoral convention, Pan appears frequently in *S.C.* as the god of shepherds (cf. Jan. 67; June 30; Nov. 8, 10; Dec. 7–12). Dec. 7–12 is fullest, where Sp. is following Marot, *Eclogue au Roy* 6–8, "O Pan, Dieu souverain Qui de guarder ne fus onc paresseux Parcs et brabis et les maistres d'iceux." Pan, in his traditional character, pipes and dances with the nymphs (June 30); cf. Theocritus 1.3; *Ecl.* 5.58–9. The story of his contest with Phoebus is alluded to at June 68 and is related by E.K.; cf. *Met.* 11.153–79. The simple shepherds' god came to be an allegorical symbol in one of the most allegorical of literary forms. At April 50,f., 91,f., the story of Pan and Syrinx (cf. *Met.* 1.689,f.) serves for eulogy of Elizabeth's parents; Pan is, as E.K. explains, "the most famous and victorious king . . . Henry the Eyght." In the *Eclogue au Roy,* addressed to Francis I, Marot had set the precedent for this kind of allegory. More frequently Pan represents Christ (May 54, July 49), or God (May 111, July 94), or the Pope (July 179), "whom they account their God and greatest shepherd." E.K.'s gloss on May 54 supplies illustrative material on this tradition. The story of Thamus, told there, appears first in Plutarch, *De Defectu Oraculorum* 17, is paraphrased with a Christian interpretation by Eusebius, *De Praeparat. Evang.* 5.17, and appears also in Gesner's *Fischbuch,* p. 106. E.K.'s whole note, with the citations, comes, as Renwick says (*S.C.,*p. 196) from Lavater, *Of Ghostes and spirites walking by night* . . . (ed. Wilson and Yardley, pp. 94–5). With Sp.'s use of Pan as Christ cf. also Boccaccio, *Eclogue* 14.23, 77; Mantuan 4.184, and Marot, *Complainct d'un Pastoureau Chrestien* ("Dressant sa plaincte à Dieu, soulz la personne de Pan"). No explanation appears for the peculiar twist which Sp. gives (2.9.40) to the story of Pan and his daughter Jynx, whom Juno (Sp. says Pan) turned into a bird; cf. Todd 4.67.

PANDIONIAN MAIDS *V.G.* 401. See *Philomela.*

PANDORA *T.M.* 578; *R.R.* 19; *Am.* 24.

R.R. 19 translates *Ant. Rome* 19.1–8. At *T.M.* 578, where Sp. calls Elizabeth "the true Pandora of all heavenly graces," he is simply playing on the meaning of her name. There is a closer adaptation of Pandora's myth at *Am.* 24. The ultimate source here is Hesiod, *Theog.* 571,f. or *Works and Days* 60,f. (S); the same story is in N.C., 4.6, who quotes Hesiod. In both authorities, the creation of Pandora came as a result of Jove's wrath at Prometheus and his desire for revenge on man; in Sp. she is a scourge for the faults of men.

PANOPE 3.8.37, 38; 4.11.49.

At 4.11.49 Panope appears, without characterization, in the list of Nereids. Sp.'s use of her at 3.8.37, 38 is quite independent, but he had precedent for doing what he liked with a sea-nymph in Lucian, *Dial. of the Sea-Gods* 5. Florimell, alone in the house of Proteus, needed a duenna; naturally Proteus, unmarried, had a housekeeper; it was logical that the person who filled both offices should be an "old nymph, hight Panope."

PARIS *S.C.* July 145, Aug. 138; *V.G.* 530; 2.7.55; 3.9.34–36; 4.1.22; 4.11.19; 6.9.36.

By scattered references, but especially at 3.9.34–36, Sp. shows a fairly complete knowledge of the Paris myth. In the main he is probably dependent on memories of general reading in the classics; but he would have found the information collected by Bocc., 6.22, and N.C., 6.23. 3.9.36 and 6.9.36 mention the story of Paris and Oenone; cf. *Heroides* 5. In the latter passage, "Plexippus brooke" seems to be Sp.'s own coinage. He might have found the name, applied to two persons quite unrelated to Paris, in Apollodorus 1.7.10 and 3.15.2. At 3.9.36 Sp. uses the Oenone myth as a start for his own story of Paridell's ancestry. Paridell is one of the more extreme examples of unchastity in men. Sp. is reinforcing his moral allegory by making Paris his ancestor. He has behind him a traditional interpretation of Paris as a type of such unchastity; cf. Fulgentius 2.1; Bocc. *loc. cit.*; N.C. *loc. cit.*, where he says of him, "Nature made him noble, but a little time joined him with lust." Cf. *Helen*. E.K.'s gloss on July 145–7, which tells the story of Hecuba's dream, is very close to Bocc. *loc. cit.* On 4.11.19 see *Nereus*.

PARNASSUS *S.C.* April 41; June 28, 70; July 47; *V.G.* 21; *T.M.* 58; *Ded. Son.* 5, 7; 1.10.54; 2.12.52; 6.Pr.2.

V.G. 21–2, translating *Culex* 15–16, gives the classical picture of Parnassus with its two peaks, "like two hornes"; cf. *Met.* 1.316–17, 2.221; Servius, *ad Aen.* 7.641. Parnassus is the haunt of Apollo here and at *T.M.* 58. Helicon, "the learned well" (see *Helicon*), flows from Parnassus. E.K.'s gloss on this line points to the characteristic association of Parnassus with the Muses and through them with heroic poetry and learning. The Muses' "abode the poets faine to be on Parnassus, a hill in Grece, for that in that countrye specially florished the honor of all excellent studies." These associations appear at June 70, where Parnassus is a symbol of heroic poetry as opposed to the pastoral; similarly at July 47; *Ded. Son* 5, 7, and perhaps most significantly at 6.Pr.2. In phrasing this last echoes Chaucer, *H.F.* 2.13, "Helpeth, that on Parnasso dwelle By Elicon the clere welle." At 1.10.54 Sp. groups Parnassus with the Hill of Contemplation and the Mount of Olives, and at 2.12.52 with other classical places and with Eden.

PASIPHAE 3.2.41.

An example of bestial lust. Cf. *Met.* 9.735–44; *Aen.* 6.24–6. Bocc., 4.10, tells the story and adds the moral interpretation which is in Sp.: "I think that the ancients wished to show by this myth how the vice of bestiality is caused in us."

PASITHEA 4.11.49. See *Nereids*.

PATROCLUS *H.L.* 233. See *Achilles*.

PEGASUS *R.T.* 426, 645–58; 1.9.21; 3.11.42.

On his birth (*R.T.* 647; 3.11.42) see *Medusa*. *R.T.* 645–58 is an adaptation to the eulogy of Sidney of the story of Pegasus' ascent to heaven; cf. *Theog.* 284–6; *Fasti* 3.451–8; Hyginus, *P.A.* 2.18; N.C., 9.4, who adds the comment that the winged horse was thus exalted "ad sublimum rerum speculationem." On this passage see also *Perseus. R.T.* 426 shows more specifically the connection of Pegasus with poetic inspiration. This connection grows out of the story of Pegasus' creating the fount Hippocrene by a stroke of his hoof (*Met.* 5.254–63; Vergil, *Catalepton* 9.2; *Silvae* 2.2.38); cf. T.M. 271. Sp.'s immediate source is probably Bocc. 10.27. Bocc. quotes Ovid, *loc. cit.*, substituting Castalia for Hippocrene (cf. E.K.'s gloss on April 42). At *R.T.* 421–8 Fame is almost equivalent to Pegasus and bears some of his attributes. Bocc. says, "Ego hunc equum famam rerum gestarum arbitror." Bocc. goes on to elaborate on Pegasus' connection with the Castalian spring and thereby with poetry and poetic fame. See *Helicon, Castalia*.

PELASGUS 4.11.15. See *Founders of Nations*.

PELEUS *V.G.* 481–2, 491–2; 6.10.22; 7.7.12.

V.G. 481–2 translates *Culex* 297. Reference to the marriage of Peleus and Thetis appears at *V.G.* 491–2 (translating *Culex* 300), at 6.10.22, and most fully at 7.7.12. Sp. may have known Catullus 64, but does not follow it. He may have taken from *Met.* 11.229 a suggestion for locating the wedding on Haemus Hill (Upton). The idea that Apollo sang "the spousall hymne" is found at *Il.* 24.62–3 (S) and in the quotation from a lost play of Aeschylus in Plato, *Republic* 383B.

PELIAS 4.11.14. See *Sea-Gods*.

PENELOPE *V.G.* 428–32; 5.7.39; *Am.* 23.

V.G. 428–32 is a fairly close translation of *Culex* 265–7. Sp. adds the epithet "faithful" and names Penelope where his original has "Ithaci coniunx . . . Icariotis." 5.7.39, a comparison of Britomart's meeting with Artegal with that of Penelope and Ulysses, is rather close to *Od.* 23.85–110 (Riedner, p. 38). With *Am.* 23, the familiar story of Penelope's web, cf. *Od.* 2.93–105.

PENEUS V.G. 183; 4.11.21; *Proth.* 78.

V.G. 183 translates *Culex* 119, with Bembo's reading "Peneu" for "pernix" (Plésent, p. 130; Emerson, p. 102). Peneus is among the famous rivers at the wedding of the Thames and the Medway (4.11.21). *Proth.* 78 places it in Tempe; cf. *Met.* 1.569.

PENTHESILEA 2.3.31; 3.4.2.

The mention of Penthesilea at 2.3.31 was probably suggested by *Aen*. 1.490–99, which Sp. is following in lines 1–5 of the same stanza. On the matter of Penthesilea's coming to aid Priam, Upton cites Dares, *De Excidio Troiae Historia*, cap. 36, and Caxton's redaction of the same. Sp. agrees with these in saying that Penthesilea was killed by Pyrrhus. At 3.4.2, in connection with Penthesilea, Sp. refers to Homer, who does not mention her. As S. says, Homer could then be taken "in a very broad sense to include certain extensions of his works, like the writings of Quintus Calaber" or Dares and Dictys. Cf. E.K.'s reference to Homer for un-Homeric material in the gloss on March 97.

PENTHEUS *V.G.* 171–6; 5.8.47.

Sp. does not name him, but in both passages refers to the story of his death. See *Agave* 2.

PENURY *H.L.* 53. See *Plenty*.

PERSEPHONE. *V.G.* 422; *T.M.* 164. See *Furies, Proserpina*.

PERSEUS *R.T.* 648–9.

Sp. departs from the classical version of the story when he says that Perseus was mounted on Pegasus when he freed Andromeda. He is following Bocc. 10.27: When Perseus went against Medusa, he had, among other things, "the winged horse, Pegasus"; and, "They say that Pegasus bore Bellerephon against the monster Chimera. Likewise he brought Perseus against the Gorgons."[16] Cf. *Pegasus*.

PHAEAX 4.11.15. See *Founders of Nations*.

PHAEDRA 1.5.37, 39; 5.8.43. See *Hippolytus*.

PHAETHON *T.M.* 7–12; *V.G.* 197–200; 1.4.9; 3.11.38; 5.8.40.

The familiar story of Phaethon's "rash decay" is behind all these references and is narrated rapidly and vividly in all three of the *F.Q.* passages. As sources, Sp. had *Culex* 127–30, which he translates freely at *V.G.* 197–200, and Ovid's extended account, *Met.* 1.750–2.329. He draws on *Met.* (2.311) for the lightning at *V.G.* 199, for the scorpion at 5.8.40 (*Met.* 2.195–200), and perhaps for the "fiery mouthed steeds" at 5.8.40 and 1.4.9 (*Met.* 2.153–5). At 1.4.9 the implicit moral of the story is made uppermost by comparing Lucifera to Phaethon, "proud of such glory and advancement vayne." N.C., 6.1, speaks of Phaethon as inflamed with contumely and says that the story exemplifies that "arrogance which draws everything to itself and thinks itself ignorant of nothing, which often leads men into great calami-

---

[16] This parallel was noted by C. C. Coulter, "The Genealogy of the Gods," *Vassar Medieval Studies*, 1923, p. 340.

ties," such as the one the R.C.K. narrowly escapes. When, at *T.M.* 7–12, Sp. speaks of the lament of the Muses for Phaethon, their brother, he is apparently identifying them with the Heliades, as daughters of Apollo, the Sun; see *Muses.*

PHAO, PHERUSA 4.11.49. See *Nereids.*

PHILOMELA *S.C.* Aug. 184–6, Nov. 141; *V.G.* 401–8; *T.M.* 236; *Daph.* 475–6.

V.G. 401–8 expands *Culex* 251–3, drawing on *Met.* 6.424–674 to explain the allusion. Sp. translates "epops" as "lapwing." For this he may depend on Gascoigne's *The Complainte of Philomene"* (1576, *Works,* ed. Hazlitt, 2.219–252). Gascoigne puts emphasis on Tereus' transformation into a lapwing. Cf. E.K.'s gloss on Nov. 141. The other references are to Philomela (at *Daph.* 475 called Philumene, as in Gascoigne) as the nightingale.

PHILYRA 3.11.43; 7.7.40.

At 7.7.40 Chiron is said to be the son of Saturn and Nais. Chiron is, in classical tradition, the son of Saturn and Philyra (*Theog.* 1001–2; *Met.* 6.126). A reference to Philyra as Nais may have been suggested by Ap. Rh. 4.813 (S) where Philyra appears among the Naiads. On 3.11.43 see *Erigone.*

PHLEGETHON *V.G.* 441, 622; 1.5.33; 2.4.41; 2.6.50; 4.2.1.

Aen. 6.550–1 (S) explains Sp.'s use of such phrases as "fiery flood" (1.5.33), "flaming" (2.6.50), "quenchless flames" (*V.G.* 622). Sp. probably also had the etymology of the name in mind, on which he would find discussion in Bocc. 3.16. But having "the damned ghosts in torment fry" (1.5.33) in Phlegethon is not according to the more usual classical tradition. This may have been suggested by N.C. 3.Pr., p. 185, "Phlegethon, rolled round with thundering waves of flames, embraces the soul," or by Dante, who has the damned souls immersed in the infernal rivers; cf. *Inferno* 14.131 and 17.1,f. In conceiving of Phlegethon as a personal deity and in using him as an ancestor of Pyrochles and Cymochles (2.4.41), Sp. may have been influenced by Bocc. 1.14 and 3.16. Bocc. fits Phlegethon into a genealogy and, in his interpretation of each of the infernal rivers as a state of the soul during its course in sin, says that Phlegethon represents Fury. This would render Phlegethon more appropriate to the allegory behind the passage.

PHLEGRA *V.G.* 39–40; 2.10.3; 5.7.10. See *Giants.*

PHOEBE See *Diana.*

PHOEBUS See *Apollo.*

PHOENIX 4.11.15. See *Founders of Nations.*

PHOLOE 1.6.15.

A nymph loved by Silvanus. Sp. is working freely; he may have known *Silvae* 2.3.8–11, where she is a nymph loved by Pan.

PHORCYS 4.11.13. See *Sea-Gods.*

PHRIXUS 5.Pr.5. See *Helle.*

PHRYGIAN MOTHER *R.R.* 6. See *Cybele.*

PHYLLIS *V.G.* 201–3. See *Demophoon.*

PIERIA *R.T.* 394; *V.G.* 25–6.

At *V.G.* 25–6, where the Naiads, "which the glorie be Of the Pierian streams," are identified with the Muses, Sp. is translating *Culex* 18–19; see *Naiads.* At *R.T.* 394 the Muses are called "Pierian sacred sisters"; cf. *Ecl.* 8.63, 9.33; *Ciris* 93.

PINDUS 3.4.41; *Proth.* 40.

Sp. knows Pindus for the whiteness of its snow (*Proth.* 40) and as the place where Apollo wooed Liagore and taught her leechcraft (3.4.41). In the second passage he may have received a suggestion from *Met.* 7.225, where Pindus is mentioned as famous for its herbs. He would have found it named as a famous mountain at *Met.* 1.570, 2.225, 11.554; *Ecl.* 10.11; Horace, *Odes* 1.12.6.

PIRITHOUS 4.10.27. See *Theseus.*

PLEASURE 3.6.50–51; *H.L.* 287–93. See *Psyche.*

PLENTY *H.L.* 50–56.

Sp. is here following the habit of Renaissance Neo-Platonists of combining and trying to harmonize the conflicting myths of Cupid's birth contained in the different speeches of Plato's *Symposium.* In the present instance Sp. is probably following N.C., 4.14, p. 398, who retells Plato's story (*Symposium* 203) and then, like Sp., connects it with the more familiar myth of Cupid as the son of Venus: "Porus, consilii et abundantiae Deus, fertur . . . Peniam deam paupertatis in horto Iovis invenisse, quam etiam compressit: ex quo igitur congressu Cupidinem postea peperit, quem Veneri famulum tradiderunt, cuius nutum mandataque observeret; *quare postea creditus est Veneris filius.*" The suggestion for introducing Plenty and Penury at this point may come from Benivieni, *Canzona,* st. 3 (cf. J.B. Fletcher, "Benivieni's 'Ode of Love' and Spenser's 'Fowre Hymnes,' " *MP,* 8.545–60), but Benivieni does not fuse the two myths as do Sp. and N.C.

> Amor . . .
> D'inopia nato et di richezza alhora
> Che di se il ciel facea, chi Cypri honora.

PLUTO *S.C.* Oct. 29; 1.1.37; 1.4.11; 1.5.14; 2.7.21; 2.7.24; 4.3.13; 4.10.58; 6.12.35; 7.7.3; cf. 2.7.3,f.

Sp.'s Pluto is in accord with the classical conception; but he does not appear in any detailed characterization. He is the husband of Proserpina (1.1.37; 1.4.11; 7.7.3; see *Proserpina*) and king of Hades (*S.C.* Oct. 29; 1.5.14; 2.7.21; 2.7.24; 4.3.13; 6.12.35). In Bocc. 8.6 and N.C. 2.9 Pluto is, in one aspect, by confusion with Plutus, the avaricious god of riches. Both dilate on the connection of wealth with underground regions and of avarice with death. This interpretation of Pluto has probably influenced Sp.'s treatment of Mammon. In 2.7.21,f. he seems to have used Bocc.'s discussion of the house of Dis and the allegory of avarice which he reads into it. See *Hades*.

PODALYRIUS 6.6.1.

Not even "that immortall spright of Podalyrius" could heal "the poysonous sting, which infamy Infixeth in the name of noble wight." Podalyrius as a famous healer is in accord with classical tradition, in which he was the son of Aesculapius and renowned for his feats of leechcraft; cf. *Il.* 2.732 (S); Diodorus 4.71; N.C. 4.11.

POLLENTE 5.2.4,f. See *Giants*.

POLLUX See *Castor*.

POLYHYMNIA *T.M.* 541–600. See *Muses*.

POLYNEICES *V.G.* 409–16. See *Eteocles*.

POLYNOME, PONTOPOREA, PORIS 4.11.49, 50. See *Nereids*.

PRIAM 2.3.31; 2.9.48; 3.9.36, 38; 4.11.19.

Troy is referred to as the city or realm of Priam at 2.9.48; 3.9.36, 38; 4.11.19. On 2.3.31 see *Penthesilea*.

PROCNE *V.G.* 401–8. See *Philomela*.

PROCRUSTES 7.6.29

Procrustes is mentioned as among those punished by Jove for trying to lay claim to heaven. There is no authority in classical tradition for such a conception. Sp. may be thinking of him somewhat vaguely as a rebellious giant and so fit company for Typhon, Ixion, and Prometheus.

PROMETHEUS 2.10.70; 7.6.29.

Sp.'s account of Prometheus' creation of man (2.10.70) differs from the most common classical versions. However, Horace, *Odes* 1.16.13–6 (S) contains something like Sp.'s idea that man was "of many parts of beasts derived." But in this particular and in the account as a whole, Sp. is closest to N.C. 4.6: Prometheus, in the creation of man, took various portions from different animals. "Qui vero etiam magis fabulose rem aggressi sunt explicare, dixerunt timorem leporis, astutiam vulpis, pavonis ambitionem, tigridem feritatem, leonum iracundiam et magnitudinem animi fuisse hominibus ab ipso Prometheo iniunctas." He then quotes Horace, *loc. cit.* But, he continues, Prometheus had left his creation without a mind. For this he stole fire from heaven and, as punishment, was chained on the Caucasus, his liver eaten by an eagle. At 7.6.29 Prometheus is mentioned among the prominent rebels against Jove, now in punishment.

PRONAEA 4.11.50. See *Nereids*.

PROSERPINA *R.T.* 373; *V.G.* 422, 461–4; *T.M.* 164; 1.1.37; 1.2.2; 1.4.11; 2.7.53,f.; 3.11.1; 3.11.35; 7.7.3.

Persephone (see *V.G.* 422, *T.M.* 164; E.K. on Nov. 164) seems to have been, for Sp., one of the Furies and so distinct from Proserpina. See *Furies*. But there is a good deal of affinity between the Furies and Proserpina herself. Jealousy (3.11.1) was brought by a Fury "from baleful house of Proserpine." At 1.2.2, the threat of "sad Proserpines wrath" reminds one of the office of the Furies. In both passages Sp. may have been influenced by *V.G.* 422–3 (which translates *Culex* 261) and by N.C. 3.16, "Hecaten sororem Eumenidum et Proserpinam poeta nominavit." As queen of Hades she appears at *R.T.* 373; 1.1.37; 1.4.11; 3.11.1; 7.7.3; *V.G.* 461–4; cf. *Theog.* 768; *Aen.* 6.138; *Theb.* 4.520,f. Proserpina is the "Thracian maid" to whom Jove appeared in the form of a serpent (3.11.35). Sp. is here following *Met.* 6.114, "varius Deoida serpens." He would have found the allusion explained by Regius (Burmann 2.389): "Deois Proserpina est, Cereris filia." On the epithet "Thracian" see Todd 5.91. By an original adaptation of myth, Lucifera, queen of Pride, becomes the daughter of Pluto and Proserpina (1.4.11). Sp. may have got a suggestion for this from N.C. 3.15: "Hanc eandem esse Proserpinam et Hecaten et Lunam credidit, quare *Lucifera* dicta est ab Euripide in Helena." In the passage on the Garden of Proserpina (2.7.51,f.), a "garden goodly garnished," but with fruits "direful dedly black," with the tree bearing the golden apples, symbols of avarice and discord, Sp. is adapting myth in the freeest sort of manner. The original suggestion probably came from Claudian, *R.P.* 2.285,f., where Pluto describes such a tree in the garden which shall be the delight of his future queen. The emphasis on gold throughout Claudian's description may have helped to suggest Sp.'s symbolism. N.C.'s comments (7.7) on the apples of the Hesperides (mentioned at 2.7.54) fit Sp.'s purpose and probably also afforded him suggestions (cf. Lemmi, p. 277): "Serpentes illi servant aurea poma qui *ob avaritiam* neque dormire . . . possunt. Quare praeclare dictum est a sapientibus divitias tanquam lapidem indicem animi cuiusquam esse datas hominibus. . . ."

PROTEUS 1.2.10; 3.4.25,f.; 3.8.30,f.; 3.8.41; 4.11.2–3; 4.12.3; 4.12.14; 4.12.41,f.; *CCCHA* 248–50.

Sp. is in accord with classical tradition when he makes Proteus a prophet and diviner (3.4.25,f.), cf. *Od*. 4.349; *Geo*. 4.392–3; *Met*. 11.249–56. His rôle as "shepherd of the seas" (3.8.30; *CCCHA* 249) probably derives from *Geo*. 4.387–95. Sp's Proteus also shares with his classical prototype, and with other sea-deities, the ability to assume many various shapes; cf. *Od*. 4.456–8; *Geo*. 4.406–10; *Met*. 8.731–7. At 1.2.10 Archimago is said to have this Protean faculty through magic art; cf. N.C. 8.8, "Alii crediderunt per magicas artes Proteum in praedictas formas se mutasse." Sp. has carried over the same idea in his treatment of Malengin (5.9.17). It is used most significantly at 3.8.39–41, where Proteus is wooing Florimell. There is no satisfactory explanation in the traditional character of Proteus for his behavior toward Florimell. It may be that Sp. is simply developing suggestions in the idea of his changeability. He may have found a hint in Bocc.'s statement (7.9) that the many shapes assumed by Proteus indicate passions: "Formas vero, quas eum sumere consuetum aiunt, et abicere, eas existimo *passiones*, quibus anguntur homines eius rei similitudinem gerentes, cui possunt merito similari."

PROTO, PROTOMEDAEA, PSAMATHE 4.11.48, 49, 51. See *Nereids*.

PSYCHE *Mui*. 131–3; 3.6.50, 51.

Both passages draw on the story of Cupid and Psyche. Sp. singles out the more important elements. From his very brief treatment, it is impossible to decide whether he knew Apuleius, *Metamorphoses* 5, 6, at first hand or used Bocc.'s rather full paraphrase of it (5.22). However, the allegorical meaning, while implicit in Apuleius, is clearly developed by Bocc. and fits Sp.'s intention at 3.6.50, 51. Bocc. says. "Psyche is the soul . . . and there is joined with her that which preserves the divine rational element, that is, pure Love." Psyche passes through trials and purgations. "At length . . . she attains to the consummation of divine joy and contemplation, and is joined to her lover forever, and, with mortal things sloughed off, is born into eternal glory; and from this love is born Pleasure which is eternal joy and gladness." Pleasure, so interpreted, is very similar to Plato's "Eudaimonia"; it is she with whom the Platonic lovers commune (*H.L.* 287–93). In the light of such an interpretation, it is fitting that she should be made Amoret's companion when the latter is educated by Psyche "in all the lore of love and goodly womanhead" (3.6.51).

PYLADES 4.10.27. See *Orestes*.

PYRACMON 4.5.37. See *Brontes*.

PYRRHA 5.Pr.2. See *Deucalion*.

PYRRHUS 2.3.31. See *Penthesilea*.

RAM See *Helle* and "Aries" under *Zodiac*.

REMUS *V.B.* 6, 9. See *Romulus*.

RHESUS *V.G.* 535.

This reference to "Strymonian Rhesus," king of Thrace, translates *Culex* 328. Cf. *Il.* 10.469 (S) and *Aen.* 1.469–73.

RHODOPE 2.12.52.

Sp. seems to be alluding to the rather obscure story of Rhodope and Haemus, but no real analogue to his version appears. *Met.* 6.87–9 refers to the myth. Regius' note on this passage (Burmann 2.386) appears to be the closest thing to Sp. It explains that Rhodope was the daughter of Haemus, a powerful king of Thrace. Neptune loved her and begat a giant. Swollen with arrogance, she called herself Juno and ordered the gods to worship her. For this she was turned into a mountain.

ROMULUS *V.B.* 6, 9; 1.5.49; 3.9.43.

Both *V.B.* passages, based on *Songe* 6, 9, refer to Romulus and Remus as infants fostered by the wolf. At 3.9.43 Romulus appears in the brief genealogical history of the descendents of Troy and founders of Britain. In putting Romulus, among the "antique ruins of the Romanes fall" (1.5.49), Sp. may have been influenced by his early translations. In *Songe* he found the Roman power and its sudden fall interpreted in a series of emblems. In *Ant. Rome* (cf. especially 12, *R.R.* 12) he found the idea that the Romans, like the giants of old, lifted too high their "haughtie front" so that the gods were afraid and struck them down. Cf. also *R.R.* 9 and *V.G.* 552–60.

SAO 4.11.48. See *Nereids*.

SATURN *V.B.* 9; *M.H.T.* 150–1; 3.11.43; 5.Pr.9; 7.6.2; 7.6.27, 34; 7.7.40; 7.7.52.

Saturn is the son of Uranus (7.6.27) and the father of Jove (7.6.2); see *Titan*. He appealed to Sp. especially as the ruler of the earth during the Golden Age (*M.H.T.* 150; 5.Pr.9). The description of the Golden Age at 5.Pr.9 is entirely in the classical tradition; cf. *Met.* 1.89–112; *Ecl.* 4; Tibullus 1.3.35,f.; *Works and Days* 109–20; cf. *Astraea*. Saturn in his astrological character, as "crabbed," ill-disposed, awful, engendering melancholy, appears at *V.B.* 7; 2.9.52; 3.11.43; 7.7.52. This aspect of him is found in classical literature (cf. Horace, *Odes* 2.17.22–3), but is more characteristically medieval; cf. Chaucer, *Kn. Tale* A 2445. Sp. would have found the same thing in Bocc. 8.1 and N.C. 2.2.

SATYRS *T.M.* 268; *V.G.* 178; *V.B.* 12; 1.6.7,f.; 3.10.36,f.; 3.11.35; 7.6.39; *Daph.* 155–61.

Satyrane was born of the union of Thyamis and a satyr who, "kindling coles of lust in brutish eye . . . made her person thrall unto his beastly kind" (1.6.22).

Here is the most distinct manifestation of the tradition which saw the satyrs as symbols of the lustful, brutish side of nature. Bocc., 8.13, says that they are part men, part "animalia bruta." N.C., 5.7, gives an etymology: "Dicti sunt autem satyri a salicitate, ut ait Theocriti enarrator, cum σάθη tentigo sit et titillatio ad Venerem." The association of brutish nature with ignorance, natural to a Platonist, appears in the use of satyrs at *T.M.* 265–82; cf. also *V.B.* 12, where Sp. substitutes satyrs for the fauns mentioned in *Songe* 12. *Daph.* 155–61, where a "cruell Satyre" is a symbol of death, may be thought of as an extension of the same idea, the destructive power of brute nature. The satyrs are in character in the Hellenore episode (3.10.36,f.). When Sp. says that they made Hellenore their "May Lady," he seems to be associating them with the fairy mythology and survivals of paganism in his own land; cf. also *V.G.* 178–9 and 1.6.7. The most extended and significant passage on the satyrs is in 1.6. Here they are somewhat more attractive. If a source is needed for the idea that they should instinctively worship Una's beauty and, without understanding her as Truth, should make her "the image of idolatries" (1.6.19), it may be in N.C., 10, p. 1033 (cited by Lemmi, p. 275), who says that the ancients made the fable of Pan as son of Mercury "cum vellent rursus demonstrare omnia naturalia corpora divinae naturae subiici, et ab illa pro sua voluntate gubernari. . . ." Cf. *Fauns;* on 3.11.35 see *Antiope.*

SCORPION 2.2.46; 5.8.40; 7.7.39. See *Orion, Zodiac.*

SCYLLA *V.G.* 539–44; 2.12.3–9.

The *V.G.* passage follows *Culex* 331–3, with slight elaboration for greater vividness. Throughout Sp.'s own version of the classical epic voyage (2.12.3,f.), in which Scylla and Charybdis appear thinly disguised as the Rock of Vile Reproach and the Gulf of Greediness, he had in mind the voyages of Odysseus (*Od.* 12.37,f.), the Argonauts (Ap. Rh. 4.789,f.), and Aeneas (*Aen.* 3.420,f.); but it seems significant that nearly all Sp.'s affinities with these passages are with such parts of them as are quoted by N.C., 8.12. Some of the parallels in descriptive detail may be noted. St. 3.5–9 echoes *Aen.* 3.421–3, quoted by N.C., p. 866. St. 4.1–4: N.C., p. 867, "Scylla promontorium est in mare prominens . . .sub ipso promontorio petrae sunt ingentes et complures, quae locos concavos et speluncas habent interius." St. 7, Scylla littered with shattered ships and carcasses of men: N.C., p. 867, "quicunque appulissent in eo, faciebant naufragium, hominesque . . . vorabuntur." St. 8, "nor fish nor fowle" approach it: *Od.* 12.62–4. Implicit throughout the passage and explicit in st. 9 is the allegory of the course of the continent man between the extremes of temptation. Sp.'s symbolism was ready made for him, most completely worked out in the spirit of his own meaning by N.C., *loc. cit.:* "Hoc quid aliud significant, quam quod scribitur ab Aristotele in Ethicis, virtutem esse medium duorum extremorum, quae ambo sunt vitanda? Ut autem vitia devitaremus extrema, his partim foemineas formas ut invitantibus ad se, tribuerunt, partim figuras immanissimarum ferarum: quippe cum eo accedentibus calamitates proponerent, et vitae et facultatum iacturam, cum canes et varia monstra horribilia (cf. 2.12.22–26) his adiunxerint, quae inhaerentes vorarent. Nam quid aliud est vita mortalium quam assidua inter varias molestias et illegitimas voluptates navigatio, . . . cum vellent igitur demonstrare antiqui . . . plenissimam esse difficultatum et periculorim vitam humanam, navigantique inter duos gravissimmos scopulos simillimam, quae si parum sapienter gubernetur, voluptatibus allecti homines in maximas miserias incident . . . ." (p. 868).

SEA-GODS 4.11.12–14.

Detailed comparison bears out the validity of Upton's and S.'s references to N.C. (2.8) as the main source of these stanzas. N.C. has all the names that appear here, except Glaucus. Sp. agrees with N.C. in making them all sons of Neptune and Amphitrite. In two places where N.C. gives detailed characterization, Sp. follows him closely. On Euphoemus he says (p. 166), "cui munus dedit *ut super undis tanquam super terra proficisceretur,*" which Sp. translates at st. 14.5–6. Again, of Astraeus, N.C. says (p. 166), "qui *per inscitiam congressus cum* Alcippa *sorore,* . . ."; cf. st. 13.7–8. But Sp. has, as in his other lists, gone beyond N.C. for some of his characterizations. On Glaucus S. cites Ap. Rh. 1.1310–11, where he appears as a prophet, as in Sp. *Aen.* 5.823, which mentions Glaucus in a passage on Neptune that Sp. uses at 3.11.40–41, may have suggested the inclusion of him in the present list. Phorcys: the reference to his "fatall brood" suggests *Theog.* 270–336; see *Medusa.* Cteatus, Eurytus: Sp. may be filling in from the meaning of their names: "rich Cteatus," κτεατίζω, κτῆμα. "Eurytus long," perhaps developed from the first part, εὑρύ. Chrysaor: his birth with Pegasus from the blood of Medusa is told at *Theog.* 281; N.C. 7.11. Eryx: cf. *Aen.* 5.392,f., 402, "acer Eryx." Asopus: S. cites a story in Apollodorus (3.12.6) to explain the line, but an intended reference to a myth hardly need be assumed. See *Brontes, Orion, Palaemon.*

SEMELE 3.11.33.

The story of Jove's love is told at *Met.* 3.259–309 (S). Semele is not in the list at *Met.* 6.103,f., which Sp. is using for most of this passage. N.C., 5.13, gives a condensed version, following Ovid, *loc. cit.,* whom he quotes. He gives everything Sp. has and a verbal parallel in ". . . si Iupiter *cum maiestate* ad eam accessisset. . . ."; cf. st. 33.3.

SIRENS See *Mermaids.*

SIRIUS *S.C.* July 22; *M.H.T.* 5; *R.R.* 26; 1.3.31. See *Orion.*

SISYPHUS *V.G.* 389–92; 1.5.35.

Among the numerous and varying versions of Sisyphus' rascalities, Sp.'s, at *V.G.* 389–92, seems to be unique. He is elaborating *Culex* 244, "contempsisse numina." Hygin., *Fab.* 60 and Horace, *Epodes* 17.68–9 are closest to Sp., but neither gives a definite cause for the punishment. At 1.5.35 Sp. simply describes Sisyphus' punishments in general terms which might come from any source; cf. *Met.* 4.460; *Od.* 16.593–600.

SLEEP 1.1.40; 2.7.25; 6.8.34; 7.7.44. See *Morpheus, Hades.*

SLOTH *T.M.* 263. See *Ignorance.*

SORROW 2.7.22. See *Hades.*

SPHINX 5.11.23–25.

The beast within the image erected by Geryoneo is, like the Sphinx, born of Typhaon and Echidna and is compared to the Sphinx, who killed herself "for very hearts despight" when Oedipus answered her riddle. Sp. has taken over N.C.'s description of the Sphinx (9.18) and applied it to his own monster: "Caput et manus puellae, corpus canis, vocem hominis, caudam draconis, leonis ungues, alas avis , . . . cum alas haberet aquilae, citissimeque ad illos convolaret . . ." The kinship is inward as well. The monster represents the Inquisition; a wrong answer to the Sphinx's riddle means death.

SPIGHT *T.M.* 317. See *Ignorance.*

SPIO 4.11.48. See *Nereids.*

STHENOBEA 1.5.50.

Sp. alludes here to the story told by Hyginus, *Fab.* 57 (S) of Sthenobea's love for Bellerephon, his refusal, her attempt to do away with him by lying to her husband, and of her killing herself when she heard that he had married someone else. Her suicide "with wilfull chord" remains unexplained; cf. Riedner, p. 45.

STYX *V.G.* 383; *R.R.* 15; 1.1.37; 1.4.48; 1.5.10; 2.5.22; 2.8.20; 3.2.52; 3.6.24; 3.7.12; 4.11.4; 5.11.32; 6.1.8; 6.6.9.

At 3.6.24 and 4.11.4 Styx is personified as the "grandame of the gods." Bocc., 3.14, calls her "Deorum nutrix et hospita." At 3.6.24 there is also the classical idea that oaths which the gods swear by Styx are irrevocable, for the gods fear her; cf. *Od.* 5.185–6; *Aen.* 6.323–4. Sp.'s conception of Styx as a river is not very clear. With his rather indiscriminate use of "lake" (2.5.21) and "swamp" or "fen" (6.1.8) cf. Vergil's "Stygiam paludem" (*Aen.* 6.323, 369), which is carried over by Bocc., 3.14. At 2.5.22 Styx is confused with Phlegethon and at *R.T.* 428; *V.G.* 338; 1.3.36 with Lethe (see *Lethe*). But several elements of the classical conception, sometimes tinged with later influences, are apparent. The epithet "loathed" (5.11.32) preserves the Greek meaning of the name; cf. N.C. 3.2, "Styx odium est" and its waters are "odiosae." Styx as the place where waiting souls pass over into Hades figures several times. At *R.R.* 15 the idea that the river is "not passable to souls returning" comes from *Ant. Rome* 15; Sp. may also have remembered Vergil's "inremeabiles undae" (*Aen.* 6.425). The classical idea that souls must wait until burial rites have been performed appears at 3.2.52 and 3.7.14; cf. *Aen.* 6.318. At 1.4.48 this is combined with the revenge motif; Sansfoy is "wandering on Stygian shores," calling for revenge. Arthur's sword, Morddure, was "seven times dipped in the bitter wave Of hellish Styx, which hidden virtue to it gave" (2.8.20); cf. *Aen.* 12.90–1 (Riedner, p. 82) and Kitchin's note, ed. *F.Q. II*, p. 213.

SYLVANUS 1.6.7,f.

Sp.'s Sylvanus, god of Satyrs and Fauns, is represented as old, infirm, leaning on a cypress staff, but a lover. Latin poets describe him as old and shaggy, but not necessarily infirm; cf. *Geo.* 1.20, 2.493–4; Horace, *Odes* 3.29.22–3 (with which cf. 1.6.7.9). On the "Sylvanes" (*S.C.* July 78) E.K. says, "of poets feigned to be gods of the woods." Cf. *Met.* 1.193.

SYRINX *S.C.* April 50,f., 90,f.

The story of Pan and Syrinx, used here, is told at *Met.* 1.689–712. Ovid's description of Syrinx as very like Diana would help to make more appropriate Sp.'s use of the myth here in connection with Queen Elizabeth. E.K.'s gloss on April 50 is also based on Ovid.

TALUS 5.1.12 and 5, *passim.*

Sp. has elaborated this figure from a rather obscure creature in Cretan and Greek mythology. The principal *loci* for the Greek Talus were first cited by Warton (Todd II.xlviii-ix). Tradition represents him as a live creature of bronze, made by Hephaestus and given to Minos, who used him as a guard of the island of Crete (cf. Roscher, *s.v. Talos*). He was noted for his swiftness and nimbleness. As the bronze guard he appears in Ap. Rh. 4.1638,f., where a version of his death is related. The classical passage which is closest to Sp. is in the pseudo-Platonic *Minos*, 320C (cf. Todd, *loc. cit.* and Gough, p. 171). Here he is "a guardian of the law," who patrolled Crete and "carried with him the laws, written in tablets of bronze; whence he was called 'the man of bronze.' " This is the most probable direct source of Sp.'s conception. One suggestion may be made as to how he happened to use it. When Astraea left the world, she left "her groom, an yron man . . . to execute her stedfast doom" (5.1.12). N.C., 2.2, says that when Astraea departed she left behind her a "testamentum" of laws. The *Minos* passage emphasizes Talus' bronze tablet. This tablet, or "testamentum," may have been the connecting link in Sp.'s mind, between Astraea and Talus. Considering Sp.'s habitual use of "iron" to denote just such qualities as his Talus possesses, it is not surprising to find him changing the tradition in this particular. He may, too, have been aware of the etymology of Greek name and its connection with τλάω; cf. "Immoveable, resistless, without end" (5.1.12).

TANTALUS *V.G.* 385–8, 546; 1.5.35; 2.7.57–60.

Tantalus is mentioned as an ancestor of Agamemnon and as one suffering punishment in Hades. In both *V.G.* passages Sp. is following *Culex* (240–2, 334) fairly closely. At 1.5.35 the phrase "hong by the chin" remains unexplained. Tantalus' most prominent appearance is at 2.7.57–60. The description of him there is fairly close to *Od.* 11.582–92 (S). In choosing him as a type to fit the allegory of avarice and greed, Sp. was probably influenced by Bocc. 1.14 (a passage which he used elsewhere; see *Theseus*): "Per Tantalum autem inter undas et *poma* (cf. st. 56) fame pereuntem, *avarorum hominum curas et agonas per infamem parsimoniam intelligere debemus.*" N.C., 6.18, also interprets him as a type of avarice, and also affords explanation for the statement at st. 59.6 that Jove was in the habit of being entertained by Tantalus, rather than the other way around, as more usually in the classical story (cf. S.): "Fuerunt qui dixerint deos aliquando in hospitum ab hoc fuisse acceptos, qui lautum convivium illis parasset."

TARTARUS *V.G.* 444, 543; 1.7.44; 2.12.6:

V.G. 444 follows *Culex* 274–5. At *V.G.* 543 Sp. fuses *Culex's* "pallentes lacus et squalida Tartara" (333) into "squalid lakes of Tartarie." He is probably thinking of Tartarus as a general name for Hades here and at 1.7.44; cf. *Aen.* 6.134–5. Mention of the "dark dreadfull hole of Tartare steepe" (2.12.6) may represent a memory of *V.G.* 542–3, where, as here, Tartarus and Charybdis are associated.

TELAMON *V.G.* 482. See *Ajax.*

TEMPE *V.G.* 144; 2.12.52; *Epith.* 308; *Proth.* 79.

V.G. 144 translates *Culex* 94–5. At 2.12.52 Tempe, where Apollo wooed Daphne, is compared to the Bowre of Blis and at *Proth.* 79 there is a brief description of the place. With both passages cf. *Met.* 1.568,f., where the story of Daphne is told with Tempe as the setting. *Epith.* 308, where Sp. makes Tempe the haunt of Maia, seems to be original with him; cf. Van Winkle, p. 115.

TEREUS *S.C.* Aug. 184–6; *V.G.* 404–8. See *Philomela.*

TERPSICHORE *T.M.* 301–360. See *Muses.*

TETHYS *R.R.* 20; 1.1.39; 1.3.31; 2.12.26; 4.11.18.

At 4.11.18 Ocean and Tethys are parents of "all the rest . . . which afterwards the sea and land possest." *Theog.* 337 (S) makes them parents of a numerous progeny, but Sp. is closer to N.C., 8.2., who after quoting *Theog. loc. cit.*, says of Tethys, "illa Deorum et animalium omnium mater dicta est." In the remaining references Tethys is synonymous with ocean. There is precedent for such usage at *Met.* 2.69 and *Theb.* 4.388. At *R.R.* 20 Sp. translates *Ant. Rome* 20, "de Thetis la chenue," as "Tethys bosom." Elsewhere (*R.R.* 4) he uses "Thetis" in the same sense for the ocean. He has apparently been influenced by N.C.'s (*loc. cit.*) confusion of the two deities. N.C. treats them as one person and at the same time as two and finally says, "Verum, sive Tethidem nominemus, sive Thetim, utraque dea fuit marina." See *Thetis*.

THALIA (1) *T.M.* 175–234. See *Muses*.

THALIA (2) 6.10.22. See *Graces*.

THALIA (3) 4.11.49. See *Nereids*.

THAUMANTES 5.3.25. See *Iris*.

THEMISTO 4.11.51. See *Nereids*.

THESEUS 1.5.35, 38; 4.10.27; 6.10.13.

Sp.'s references to Theseus are hardly consistent. At 1.5.35 he is in Hades, "condemned to endlesse slouth by law." Although commentators have referred this to *Aen.* 6.617-18, it is a translation of Bocc. 1.14, where he is paraphrasing *Aen. loc. cit.*, "Theseum *perpetuo damnatum otio*." At 4.10.27 Theseus and Pirithous are among the noble lovers in the garden of Venus. Their friendship was famous in classical literature and they are often mentioned together; cf. *Aen.* 6.393; *Met.* 8.303, 405–6, 12.210,f. On 6.10.13 see *Ariadne*. On 1.5.38 see *Hippolytus*. Theseus' "sea-god sire" (1.5.38) can be either his grandfather, Neptune, or his father, Aegeus, who, according to Bocc. 10.48, was also a sea-god.

THETIS *V.G.* 491–2; *R.T.* 428–9; *R.R.* 4; 4.11.48; 6.10.22; 7.7.12.

At *R.T.* 428–9 there is a version of the story of Thetis dipping Achilles in the Styx, for which Sp. substitutes Lethe; cf. E.K. on March 97 and Bocc. 12.52, which E.K. follows, and see *Lethe*. At *R.R.* 4 Thetis' name is used by metonymy for the ocean, following *Ant. Rome* 4.2. S. cites Martial 10.30 for the same usage; cf. *Tethys*. Thetis is mentioned among the fifty Nereids at 4.11.48; see *Nereids*. On *V.G.* 491–2; 6.10.22; 7.7.12, the marriage of Peleus and Thetis, see *Peleus*.

TIBER *R.R.* 13; 4.11.21.

In both passages Tiber appears as a river-god. *R.R.* 13 translates *Ant. Rome* 13. Cf. *Fasti* 5.637–62.

TIRYNTHIAN 6.12.35; *Epith.* 329. See *Hercules*.

TISIPHONE *V.G.* 342. See *Furies*.

TITAN *S.C.* July 59; 1.2.7; 1.4.8; 1.11.33; 2.3.1; 2.5.27; 2.6.31; 2.11.9; 3.4.60; 3.6.6; 4.1.16; 6.3.13; 7.6.27, 33–34; *H.H.B.* 163; *Proth.* 4.

The story of the usurpation of Titan's rights by Saturn and his son Jove (7.6.27, 33–34) is based on N.C. (S) 6.20: "The rule, by hereditary right, belonged to Titan,

Saturn's brother, because he was older." But it was arranged that Saturn should rule on condition that, if he had male children, he would kill them, so that after Saturn the power would return to Titan. "When Jove was secretly brought up, contrary to the agreement, and took over his father's kingdom, Titan and his sons took up arms and declared war against Jove, illegitimately and contrary to the oaths of their fathers. . . . With thunderbolts they were hurled down into the lower regions." In all the other references Titan appears as the sun; cf. *Met.* 1.10, 6.438, 10.79, 11.257; *Aen.* 4.119.

TITANS 2.7.41; 3.7.47; 5.1.9; 7.6.2,f.

Sp. is not explicit as to the parents of the Titans, but one may infer from 3.7.47 and 7.6.27 that he followed the classical tradition that they were born of Caelus and Terra (cf. *Theog.* 207). Nor does Sp. draw any clear distinction between Titans and Giants, though at 3.7.47 the Giants are thought of as the offspring of the Titans, a second generation. On the battle of the Titans and Giants (Sp. does not distinguish) against the Olympians, see *Giants*. For Sp., the Titans and Giants meant, above all, pride, overweening and rebellious against established order. Thus he speaks of their "presumptuous might" (*R.R.* 17), of their foolhardiness (3.11.22), of the malice of Earth in bearing them (5.7.10), of their "rebellion" (5.1.9); and the same meaning is, of course, prominent through *Mut.* Bocc., 4.1, finds in their myth a "moralem sensum naturali mixtum," to the effect that in their very birth the Titans typify revenge. "Titan, quod ut placet Lactantio, idem quod *ultio* sonat." N.C., 6.20,21 (cf. Lemmi, pp. 275–76), is more emphatic. Titans and Giants exemplify "ambitionis furor." They were justly punished for their "temeritas et avaritia." Cf. *Bellona, Hecate, Mutability, Titan.*

TITHONUS 1.2.7; 1.11.51; 3.3.20; *Epith.* 75. See *Aurora.*

TITYUS *V.G.* 377–80; 1.5.35.

In both passages Tityus appears in his conventional place as one of those punished in Hades. The *V.G.* passage, following *Culex* 237–40 with some expansion but no change of sense, gives "Latona's displeasure" as the cause. 1.5.35.6 shows a closer reading of *Aen.* 6.595–600 (Riedner, p. 79), which agrees with Sp. and differs from other classical versions in naming only one vulture.

TRIPTOLEMUS *V.G.* 208. See *Ceres.*

TRITON *Mui.* 296; 3.4.33; 4.11.12; *CCCHA* 244–7.

In the classics Triton appears habitually as Neptune's first assistant in the affairs of the sea. Several extensions of this office appear in Sp. It is he who trained the dolphins that draw Cymodoce's car (3.4.33). Going before Neptune and Amphitrite at the wedding of the Thames and the Medway is Triton, blowing his trumpet "for goodlie triumph and great jolliment" (4.11.12). Cf. N.C.'s statement (8.3) that

Triton is "Oceani ac Neptuni buccinator et tubicen." He appears as the helper of Neptune in stilling the waves at *Aen.* 1.144 and *Met.* 1.333. The latter passage is the source for *CCCHA* 244–7, where Triton and Proteus are the "shepherds" of Cynthia's "herds of thousand fishes"; cf. *Proteus.* At *Mui.* 296 "the Tritons" sound their horns as Jove carries Europa over the sea. This is based on Moschus 2.123, "And round him were gathered the Tritons, those hoarse trumpeters of the deep, blowing on their long conches a bridal melody."

TRITONS *Mui.* 296. See *Triton.*

TRYPHON 3.4.43; 4.11.6–7; 4.12.22.

Tryphon is "the sea-gods soveraine leeche," called in to practice on Marinell. No god by this name appears in classical literature, nor, it would seem, anywhere before Sp. except in Bocc. 7.36, where the name occurs as a misreading for "Trophonius" in Cicero, *Nat. Deor.* 3.22. Bocc. says: "Cicero autem ubi de naturis (*sic*) deorum hunc Mercurium, qui *Triphon* appellatus est, filium dicit fuisse Valentis et Coronidis. Leontius autem addit, dicens eum *fratrem fuisse Aesculapii medici. . . .*" Sp. has built up his character from a mere name and from the remark that the one named was a brother of Aesculapius—hence probably a physician. The name itself, by its resemblance to Triton, is perhaps reason enough for giving it to a sea-god.

TURNUS *V.B.* 9; 3.9.42.

Both references are to the combat of Aeneas and Turnus and the latter's death. Turnus is named only at *V.B.* 9, where Sp. is translating *Songe* 9. See *Aeneas.*

TYNDARID LASS 4.11.19. See *Helen.*

TYPHAON 5.10.10; 6.6.11.

Typhaon's "tempestuous rage" (6.6.11) may be a recollection of N.C. 6.22, where he is interpreted as standing for wind. Typhaon and Echidna are the parents of Orthrus (5.10.10) and of the Blatant Beast (6.6.12); see *Orthrus, Blatant Beast.* As a personification of wind, and always linked with Echidna, Typhaon was probably distinct in Sp.'s mind from Typhon or Typhoeus.

TYPHOEUS *V.B.* 15; 1.5.35; 3.7.47–48; 7.6.15, 29.

The names Typhoeus and Typhon seem to be interchangeable in Sp., as in N.C. 6.22, and apply to one of the Giants who was most active in rebelling against Jove. This is Sp.'s chief impression of him; cf. *Geo.* 1.278–83; *Aen.* 9.716; *Met.* 3.303; *Theog.* 821,f., which is the fullest account of his exploits. N.C., *loc. cit.*, interprets his myth as showing "ambitionis furor"; cf. *Titans.* At 1.5.35 Sp. adds him to the conventional group of those eternally punished in Hades. The idea that he lies with "his joints stretched on a gin" seems to be Sp.'s own. For the story of how Typhoeus begot Argante and Ollyphant (3.7.47), Sp. may have received a suggestion from N.C.'s remark (*loc. cit.*) that all serpents and dragons are born from his blood. The reference to "Typhoeus sister" (*V.B.* 15) translates *Songe* 15; see *Bellona*.

ULYSSES *V.G.* 193–6, 429–32, 531–44; 1.3.21; *Am.* 23.

In the *V.G.* passages Sp. draws all his material from *Culex* (123–6, 265–7, 325–33). The "griesly fiends of hell" (*V.G.* 544) are Sp.'s addition, perhaps a memory of *Od.* 11. With 1.3.21, Ulysses "that for his love refused deitye," that is, who, for his longing to return to Penelope, refused to become immortal by staying with Calypso, cf. *Od.* 5.135–6, 208–9. On *V.G.* 429–32 and *Am.* 23 see *Penelope*.

URANIA *T.M.* 481–540. See *Muses*.

URANUS 7.6.27.

Uranus is mentioned as the father of Titan and Saturn. This is in accord with *Theog.* 132–8; N.C. 6.20, and Bocc. 8.1. See *Titan*.

VENUS

Sp. follows the classic myth of Venus' birth from "oceans fruitful froth" (2.12.65; 4.12.2). He probably knew this as given at *Theog.* 195–8 (S). He follows common classical usage in calling her Cytherea (*T.M.* 397; *Mui.* 397; 3.6.20; *H.B.* 260; but see *Cytheron*), and Cyprian (2.12.65; *Epith.* 103; *H.B.* 55). He mentions Cnidus as a haunt of Venus (3.6.29; cf. *Met.* 10.529–32; Horace, *Odes* 3.28.13) and knows of her temples at Cyprus (4.10.5) and Paphos (3.6.29; 4.10.5, 40). Classical descriptions of these last have probably influenced his description of her temple in 4.10.5,f. With sts. 37, 38 cf. *Aen.* 1.415–7; *Theb.* 5.61. Cf. also Bocc. 11.4, "Eique apud Paphos templum et ara fuit, eamque aram solo thure et floribus redolentem faciebant, eo quod Venus ex variis causis odoribus delectetur." Sp. may also have received a suggestion for his description of the garden and the temple from Claudian, *Epithalamium* 49,f., where there is a description of the garden and castle of Venus on Cyprus (cf. 4.10.6, "on an island"), enclosed and inaccessible but to the elect (cf. 4.10.6), the palace built of precious stones and gold (cf. 4.10.5–6); there is a plain (cf. 4.10.8) and shady groves made for lovers (cf. 4.10.25). Sp. refers three times to the portrait of Venus by Apelles (*Ded. Son.* 17; 4.5.12; *H.H.B.* 211–14); cf. Ovid, *Ars Amat.* 3.224; *Amores* 1.14.33–4; Pliny, *Nat. Hist.* 35.10 (Upton); N.C. 4.13, though none of these explains Sp.'s allusions sufficiently. Her team of sacred swans draws her through the sky (*Proth.* 62); cf. *Met.* 10.717–8 (S); Horace, *Odes* 4.1.10 (S). Venus' doves are introduced into the description of Charissa (1.10.31); cf. *Theb.* 5.63. At *Daph.* 109 the poet alludes to the story of how the rose became red from Venus' blood. The source is probably N.C. 5.16, which S. quotes without reference; cf. also *Anthologia Latina* 85, 366 (S).

Venus' "delight is all in joyfulnesse. In beds, in bowres, in banckets, and in feasts" (3.6.22). This is the Venus of most of classical literature, untouched by philosophy, Platonic or Lucretian, but perhaps associated in Sp.'s mind with the Aphrodite Pandemos of *Symposium* 180–181. Several passages seem reminiscent of the Homeric "φιλομμειδὴς Ἀφροδίτη." Thus 1.6.16, "Venus never had so sober mood," and 4.10.47, where she is called "mother of laughter"; cf. N.C. 4.13, where he translates the Homeric phrase as "Laetitiae parens Venus." Cf. also 4.10.56 and *Am*. 39, which is based on Ronsard, *Amours* 1.181 (Renwick, *Daph*., p. 200). More particularly suggestive of Venus Pandemos is the use made of her at 1.1.48 and 1.2.4, where illicit love is referred to as "Venus shameful chain"; cf. *Ecl*. 8.78, "Veneris vincula," and in general the classical use of Venus' name as synonymous with love: *Aen*. 6.26; *Geo*. 3.97, 4.199; *Met*. 3.294. With the phrase "Venus sting" (2.12.39) cf. *Geo*. 3.210. The classical Venus also presided over marriage; cf. *Il*. 5.429 (S); *Met*. 9.796, 10.295; see *V.G*. 486–8 (following *Culex* 299) and *H.L*. 283–6.

Venus' girdle, the Cestus (4.5.3–6), is a symbol of her relations to legitimate and illegitimate love. S. refers to *Il*. 14.214.21, but Sp.'s use of the Cestus is quite different from Homer's and is probably dependent on Bocc. 3.22, 4.47. Following Bocc., Sp. makes it a symbol of "wivehood true," which Venus must lay aside when she indulges in illicit love. This idea of the Cestus may start with *Theb*. 5.62–3, "iugalem Ceston," on which Lact. has a long note which is used by Bocc. at 3.22. With 4.5.3.1–2 cf. Bocc. 4.47, "Veneris cingulam est dictum Ceston, quod ipsa fert ad legitimos coitus," and 3.22, "Hoc cingulam, dicit Lactantius, . . . Venerem non ferre nisi ad honestas nuptias." With 4.5.3.7–9 cf. "Cum vero in illicitos tendit, cingulam deponit et sic illi solutis vestibus in illicitos ire coitus ostendebant" (4.47). With 4.5.4.7–8 cf. ". . . ut aliquali coertione vaga nimis lascivia frenatur" (3.22).

"Venus looking glasse" (3.1.8; 3.2.17,f.), in which Britomart sees the image of her future lover, may, as Warton says (Todd 4.305), owe something to Chaucer, *Squire's Tale* F 132–45 and to medieval lore; but it is also related to the Platonic mirror, which was a favorite image with Sp. The origin of this is in *Phaedrus* 255D (Lee). Glauce's words at 3.2.40 shows that the Platonic meaning of the mirror is intended.

We come now to Sp.'s use of Venus as a symbol of more definitely philosophical notions. In the passage on the temple of Venus (4.10.38,f.), Sp. is at several points indebted to Plutarch, *De Iside*. Venus' priestesses wear linen robes (4.10.38); so Isis' priests (Plutarch 3). The statue of Venus is covered with a veil; cf. Plutarch 8, quoted in Todd, 5.415. Here and at *CCCHA* 801 Venus is said to contain both sexes within herself; cf. Servius, *ad Aen*. 2.632 (S) and Macrobius, *Saturnalia* 3.8.1; cf. *Cupid*. This is but a mythological way of presenting Venus as *creatrix* and *genetrix*, mother and preserver of all living things. Cf. "great Mother Venus" (4.10.5; 3.6.40), "great mother" of Love (4.10.29; *H.B*. 16), "mother of delight" (*T.M*. 398), "mother of laughter" (4.10.47), "mother milde" (1. Pr.3), cause of the sea's fruitfulness (4.12.2). Something of this motherly aspect of Venus probably comes from *Aen*. (cf. 2.591; 12.411–12), but the main source is Lucretius 1.1–23, which is the basis for the lover's invocation at 4.10.44–47. Sp. is here making a free translation of this passage, but he is also using *Geo.* 2.323,f. and N.C. 4.13. On p. 395 N.C. quotes Lucretius 1.1–13 and also *Geo.* 2.323–331. In 4.10.45 Sp. seems to follow *Geo.* 2.324 in lines 3–4 and 328 in line 8. The idea in 4.10.47.1, that Venus made the world, is not in Lucretius but is in N.C.: "Venerem mundum procreasse et conservare." The phrase "queen of the aire" (4.10.47.7) may refer to the idea in N.C. that Venus "ex aeris temperie gignatur." Thus it seems quite possible that Sp. had this page of N.C. open before him when he wrote the passage. The *Geo.* lines are not primarily about Venus and so might not have occurred to him had they not been quoted there. The conception of Venus as the physical "rerum omnium procreatrix" is uppermost in the Garden of Adonis passage (3.6.30,f.) as well as in 4.10. But the presence of the Platonic lovers in her garden (4.10.26) shows that Venus is here also something more, is also the Aphrodite Ourania of Plato (*Symposium* 180–181; cf. *Phaedrus* 256B). It is this Platonic Venus primarily that Sp. intends when he speaks of the "Queen of Beauty" (*S.C.* Aug. 138; *T.M.* 138; *Ded. Son.* 17; 4.5.1; 4.5.26; 4.10.29; 4.10.44; 6.10.17; *H.B.* 15,f.). The symbolic connection of Venus with Divine Beauty probably owes something to Plato himself (cf. *Phaedrus* 250), but it was primarily the work of the Italian Neo-Platonists.[17] It was they who mystically identified Plato's Venus Urania with the Idea of Beauty and with the world of Ideas in general.[18] At 3.6.12 Venus is said to have her heavenly dwelling in "the house of goodly formes and faire aspects," that is, in the Platonic world of Ideas. At *H.B.* 29–56 she is definitely identified with the "wondrous paterne" by which the world was made; she is the Idea of Beauty. In the same passage (50,f.) she is also the celestial influence emanating from the perfect pattern of the world, creating beauty in earthly forms. This last idea is not uncommon in the Neo-Platonists already cited, but the statement of it in *H.B.* 55–63 is closest to N.C. *loc. cit.*: "Alii naturam sapientissimam rerum harum parentem similium et animorum et temperamentorum conciliatricem crediderunt: quae radios quosdam occultos e toto corpore mitteret (cf. 43–4, 54–6): quos tamen alii ex oculis manare maluerunt atque alterius animum percutere, atque illum qui sit ictus, conversum eo unde percussus fuit, quandam voluptatem divinantem, et quasi praesentientem, in eius desiderium delabi (cf. 59–61), quod desiderium Amor, et proprio nomine Cupido appellatur" (cf. 62–3). The conception of Venus as the Heavenly Idea of Beauty also lies behind *H.L.* 71–3, where, perhaps following Benivieni, *Canzona*, st. 4,[19] Sp. says that Venus lent light to Cupid as he moved out of Chaos, creating the world. In all this, and especially at *H.L.* 73 and *H.B.* 43–56, the astrological character of Venus as a planet has fused with Neo-Platonic doctrines of emanation. Venus as the personal deity of Beauty is merged with the star that is "the cause of

---

[17] Cf. J. B. Fletcher, "Benivieni's 'Ode of Love' and Spenser's 'Fowre Hymns'," *MP*, 8.545–60; Winst., *Hymnes*, especially pp. lxii–iii and 54–55 for illustrative material from Ficino and Bruno; Mrs. Bennett, "The Theme of Sp.'s *Fowre Hymnes*," *SP*, 28.18–57, for similar material from Benivieni and Pico della Mirandola.

[18] On this general identification Lee quotes Ficino 2.7. Mrs. Bennett, *op. cit.* p. 32, finds the same thing in Pico, *Commento* 2.11, and Fletcher, *op. cit.*, pp. 552–3, shows similar doctrines in Benivieni, *Canzona*, st. 5.

[19] Cf. Fletcher, *op. cit.*, p. 551.

unquietness in love" in E.K.'s gloss on Dec. 60, and Venus' star is taken as the symbol of beauty at *Daph.* 483 and *Ast.* 56. As the planet she appears also at Dec. 84; 3.6.2; 7.7.51.

On 4.5.5; 6.10.8 see *Acidalia;* on 3.1.34–38; 3.6.46–49 see *Adonis;* on 3.9.41 see *Aeneas;* on *Mui.* 113,f. see *Astery* 1; on 3.6.11,f.; 3.11.45; *CCCHA* 803,f.; *Epig.* 4; *H.L.* 24, 62, and on Venus as mother of Cupid, see *Cupid;* on *T.M.* 403; 2.8.6; 4.5.6; 6.10.9,f.; *Epith.* 103 see *Graces;* on 2.8.6 see *Ida;* on *Mui.* 371; 2.6.35; 3.6.4; 3.11.44; 4.5.5 see *Mars;* on 2.7.55; 4.1.22; *S.C.* Aug. 138 see *Paris;* on *Mui.* 128–34; 3.6.50 see *Psyche;* on *Mui.* 369; 4.5.4 see *Vulcan.*

VESPER *V.G.* 315; 7.6.9. See *Hesperus.*

VESTA 7.7.26.

Vesta is goddess of "fire aethereall." Cf. *Fasti* 6.291–2 and N.C., 8.19, who quotes this and says, "Cum igitur aeternus sit *ignis aetherius*, iure optimo Vesta aeterna vocata fuit."

VIRGO *M.H.T.* 1–4; 5.1.11; 7.7.37; *Daph.* 218. See *Astraea.*

VULCAN *Mui.* 63, 369–74; *V.B.* 4; *V.G.* 524; 2.7.5; 2.7.36; 3.9.19; 3.11.26; 4.5.4; 7.7.26.

Sp.'s use of Vulcan is entirely classical. He is the "Lemnian god" and his workshop is in "Lemno" (*Mui.* 370; 4.5.4). He is given this epithet at *Met.* 4.185; *Aen.* 8.454; *Theb.* 2.269. *Il.* 1.590–4 shows the origin of Vulcan's association with Lemnos. Vulcan is lord of material fire used by man (7.7.26) and his name is used by metonymy for fire (2.7.36; 3.9.19; *V.G.* 524); cf. *Met.* 7.104. With the use of "Mulciber" in the same way (2.7.5; 3.11.26) cf. *Met.* 9.263; *Theb.* 6.234. The reference at *V.B.* 4 to Vulcan as the forger of his father's thunderbolts is a close translation of *Songe* 4.9–11. *Mui.* 63 mentions Achilles' shield, made by Vulcan; cf. *Il.* 18.369,f.; *Aen.* 8.407,f.; *Met.* 13.288; see *Achilles.* On *Mui.* 369–74 see *Mars;* on 4.5.4 see *Venus.*

WOOD-GODS *V.G.* 178; 1.6.7; 4.11.33; 6.2.26; 7.6.35; 7.6.50; *Ast.* 50.

On *V.G.* 178 see *Pan;* on 7.6.39 see *Satyrs;* on 7.6.50 see *Fauns.* Sp. uses the term "wood-god" loosely to indicate all varieties.

WOOD-NYMPHS *V.G.* 182; 1.6.18; 2.3.28; 3.6.16; 4.7.23; 6.2.25; 7.6.39; *Epith.* 37–8; *Ast.* 43.

They are usually associated with Diana or Belphoebe; but the term is used without special reference to a particular class of nymphs. On *V.G.* 182 and 1.6.18 see *Hamadryads;* on the rest see *Nymphs.*

ZEPHIRUS 2.5.29; 2.12.33; *Proth.* 2.

Zephirus is "sweet breathing" (*Proth.* 2); his breath brings out the odors of the flowers on Phaedria's isle (2.5.29); he whistles a treble, "a strange kind of harmony" to the song of the Sirens (2.12.33). In all this Sp. is with classical usage, but he may have meant more. E.K. knows the story of Zephirus and Chloris (gloss on April 122; see *Chloris*). This story connects him with flowers and spring and the power of growth. Sp.'s references suggest that he held the same associations for him. Bocc., 4.61, says, "Zephirus ventus est occiduus, . . . humidus, temperate, . . . Hyems autem resolvit et germina floresque producit, et dicitur Zephirus a zeph quod Latine vita sonat. Favonius autem eo quod foveat germinantia, vel faveat germinibus." Further, by connecting Zephirus with the Sirens' song and with Phaedria's isle, Sp. suggests the incontinent and immoral extension of this power which is discussed by Bocc. in the same connection.

ZODIAC *S.C.* July 21, Nov. 16, Dec. 57; *M.H.T.* 6; 5.Pr.5–6; 5.1.11; 7.7.32–43; *Daph.* 165; *Epith.* 269; *Proth.* 174.

Chiefly in two passages, Sp. uses the signs of the zodiac mythologically. In the first of these (5.Pr.5–6) he uses this material to express his pressing sense of the world's change and degeneration (cf. also 7.7.47,f.). In the second (7.7.32–43) he uses it for pageantry and spectacle, with a skillful interweaving of the physical and the mythological. A review of this second passage, the procession of the months, will serve to indicate Sp.'s treatment elsewhere as well. Aries (st. 32): March, riding on a ram, the same which carried Phrixus and Helle (see *Helle*). Bocc., 4.68, discusses Aries as symbolic of procreation and the fruitfulness of spring (cf. lines 6–9). Taurus (st. 33): April, on a bull, the same that carried away Europa (see *Europa*). His horns are crowned with garlands; cf. *Met.* 2.27, 867–8.[20] Gemini (st. 34): May, carried on the shoulders of the twins of Leda; see *Castor*. Cancer (st. 35): June, riding on a crab; cf. 5.Pr.6; *Epith.* 269. Leo (st. 36): July, hot and fierce, riding on a lion which is identified with the Nemean lion (so also *Daph.* 165); cf. Hygin., *P.A.* 2.24, where the same identification is made. Cf. *S.C.* July 21, Dec. 57 (and E.K.'s glosses); *M.H.T.* 6; *Daph.* 165; 5.Pr.6. Virgo (st. 37): August leads a lovely maid; see *Astraea*. Libra (st. 38): September, holding a "knife hook" and a pair of weights; cf. 5.1.11. Scorpio (st. 39): October rides on a scorpion, "the same which by Dianaes doom unjust slew great Orion"; see *Orion*. Sagittarius (st. 40): November rides on a "dreadful centaur," Chiron, son of Saturn and "Nais"; see *Philyra*. Cf. N.C. 4.12: "Conversus est igitur Chiron in signum illud coeleste, quod nunc etiam a sagitta illa nomen retinet." Capricornus (st. 41): December, on a goat, the same wherewith the Idaean maid nourished "Dan Jove, in tender years." On the Idaean maid, Amalthea, cf. *Fasti* 5.115.f. (S) and N.C. 7.2, where he tells the story and says that the goat was put among the stars. Aquarius (st. 42): January, standing on a pot, "from whose wide mouth there flowed forth the Roman flood." It was commonly

[20] W. P. Cumming, "The Influence of Ovid's *Metamorphoses* on Spenser's 'Mutabilitie' Cantos," *SP*, 28.241–56, shows the extent of Sp.'s indebtedness to Ovid, especially in the speech of Mutability (7.7.17, f.) and in the pageant of the seasons and months (7.7.27–46). I have followed him in his references to *Met.* at this point.

held that Ganymede became Aquarius. No explanation appears for the reference to the "Roman flood." Pisces (st. 43): February, in a wagon drawn by "two fishes for the season fitting." Sp. uses no myth here.

As models for this passage as a whole, Sp. had *Met.* 2.25,f., referred to above, and probably also the fuller treatment of the same material, more nearly in the spirit in which he himself wrote, in the Induction to *The Mirror for Magistrates.*

INDEXES

INDEX OF MYTHOLOGICAL NAMES

(It has been thought necessary to index only those names which appear in the Introduction.)

INDEX OF AUTHORS